a time to burn?

a
time
to
burn?

*an
evaluation
of the
present
crisis in
race
relations*

Louis H. Masotti
*Department of Political Science
Case Western Reserve University*

Kenneth F. Seminatore
*School of Law
Harvard University*

Jeffrey K. Hadden
*Department of Sociology
Tulane University of Louisiana*

Jerome R. Corsi
*Department of Government
Harvard University*

RAND McNALLY & COMPANY • CHICAGO

CONTENTS

PREFACE

This book is addressed to white America. Its authors are white. We are not 'bleeding heart' liberals. In traditional political rhetoric, we represent a spectrum from moderately liberal to moderately conservative—though we would all agree that such traditional conceptions of political ideology have become largely irrelevant in this decade. We are scholars who, in the past several years, have become increasingly concerned about the ever deepening crisis in race relations in America.

To be sure, we are concerned about riots and their immediate impact of fear, suffering, and loss of life and property. But more importantly, we are concerned about the broader implications of violence for the future of this nation. We are concerned that the large majority of white Americans do not really understand what is happening, and in failing to understand they reinforce the likelihood, indeed the inevitability, of intensified violence.

It must be understood that what is happening has much broader implications than the nuisance of violence in streets far removed from our own. The history of the United States has been a gradual and painful realization of the implications of the Declaration of Independence. Today this unfolding realization stands in jeopardy. Whether we can meet this crisis and move on in the continuing struggle to create a free and just society is the most serious question this nation has faced in its history. The struggle between black and white is only one dimension of this crisis, but at this moment it has surfaced and in one way or another embraces all the other dimensions.

This volume is an attempt to analyze and interpret the deepening and entangling racial crisis we as a nation face. We cannot tell the story from the perspective of those who have suffered its agony and abuse—though we have tried to let black Americans speak through extensive quotations of their words. The more we know people from the dark ghettoes, the more we doubt whether we can ever know what it is like or speak effectively in their behalf. But we understand that what is happening in the ghetto has the gravest implications for what will happen throughout this nation—unless white Americans move very quickly to chart a new course. As academics, we have a commitment to, and faith in, the value of knowledge. We address ourselves to white Americans in the hope that knowledge may increase understanding, which in turn may lead to action.

We as a nation, if we can believe the public opinion polls, largely approve of the efforts of American Negroes to achieve first-class citizenship. More than once we have risen in rage to protest the brutal measures of a Bull Connor or the Klan. Except for a few regional pockets, blatant bigotry has largely been repudiated by the majority of Americans.

To be sure, the intensity of feeling for equality for Negroes, as opposed to passive acceptance, varies enormously. But even most of us who feel strongly that racial equality must be achieved are not significantly involved. We are a sympathetic ear to a liberal press, we have occasional friendly encounters with middle-class Negroes who have escaped the ghetto, and we make our modest financial contributions to the NAACP or the Urban League. But we are not really involved. Thus we have failed to understand the emerging militant mood of the ghettoes which cries 'Black Power' and 'Burn, Baby, Burn.'

We have taken pride in the progress measured in terms of civil rights legislation, poverty programs, integration of public facilities, and the highly visible presence of Negroes in business and government. Yet most of us remain blind to the inescapable evidence which indicates that all these efforts have not fundamentally altered the life chances of the large majority of American Negroes.

We lack the psychic capacity to grasp the depth of agony and frustration of a minority ignored in the midst of the most affluent society in human history. We do not understand that the majority of Negroes remain second-class citizens not so much because of the blatant bigotry of the Carl McIntyres and the Lincoln Rockwells, but rather because the majority of white Americans have been unwilling to examine the magnitude of the problem and demand action to correct the generations of abuse and discrimination which we have inherited.

Because we are only peripherally involved, we see only the progress, but fail to realize the immensity of the unfinished task. We do not know what it is like to be told that the rat-infested slums, the inferior education, and the discriminating practices of the market place are going to be eliminated, but to grow into adulthood and find that nothing has changed. What seems like a short time to us is an eternity to the Negro who is slipping from youth to adulthood without seeing his life chances altered. We don't know what it is like to have middle-class aspirations sink into despair, hopelessness, and hate.

And because we have failed to understand these things, we are incapable of grasping or responding to the angry mood of the ghetto which is raising its voice in cries of Black Power and unprecedented violence. Nor are we capable of grasping the reality of escalating violence by whites against blacks.

We continue to believe that the rioting is the work of, and reflects the sentiments of, only a very small minority of Negroes. Most Negroes, we believe, are good citizens who deplore the rioting as much as we do. That this may be true is largely irrelevant because it ignores the pace at which sentiment for violent expressions of frustration is growing.

While white America can isolate itself from the ghetto and, as a result, remain blind to its harsh realities, most of black America cannot escape. Moreover, the presence of television in even the darkest of ghettos makes it virtually impossible for them to escape awareness of the affluent other America. Indeed, television creates an image of affluence which is actually beyond the grasp of more than a small percentage of whites.

But most blacks do not know this because they have never been in white America.

Black America knows that the gulf between them and white America is large. They know that Congress and white America has turned its back on them again and again. They know that much of the legislation passed by Congress does not really affect their lives, and that where it might the mechanisms do not exist to enforce the law. They know that billions are being spent in Vietnam, which if directed to the domestic crisis might make a difference. They know that the trade unions remain stubbornly resistant to change. And they are becoming increasingly convinced that white America does not really care enough to do those things necessary to make a significant difference. With every day, week, month, in which nothing happens, they become more convinced that nothing significant is going to happen in their lifetime.

To a very great extent, riots are a cry of utter despair, pleading for someone to hear and respond. Yet our response has been more talk, more unfulfilled promises, more tokenism, and recently, more suppression. And while we are talking, the disillusionment and frustration of the ghetto is accelerating at a frightening pace. The civil rights efforts of the past decade and the continual bombardment of the mass media have heightened the consciousness and raised the expectations of the Negro far beyond the level of our response.

Those who say that the riots have nothing to do with the civil rights movement are either engaging in enormous self-delusion or are attempting to protect the good name of a phase of the movement which is more palatable to themselves and the American public. They are blind to a long history of social revolutions which have often begun as broad-based nonviolent efforts to change institutionalized injustices, only to merge as violent social revolutions when more moderate efforts failed.

As a minority of slightly more than ten per cent of the population, Negroes stand little chance of winning in a violent confrontation. But before the militant leaders push the Negro community beyond the point of no return, we must do some sober thinking about the consequences of such a confrontation. American society itself would be the ultimate loser. We would become the captives of fear and hate of a magnitude which would make Nazi Germany and apartheid South Africa seem like meccas for civil libertarians. Such a confrontation would make a mockery of the American Revolution and the entire history of our experiment in democracy. But even this might be a relatively minor consequence. In a mood of rage and hate, the balance of power in this nation might very well shift into the reckless hands of those who would disrupt the precarious balance of peace between the nuclear powers and plunge the whole world into nuclear holocaust.

These are frightening thoughts, and we would feel much more comfortable if we could dismiss them. But the fact of the matter is that the angry mood of the Negro revolt is rapidly reaching frightfully dangerous proportions. It is not going to go away if we turn on the water hydrants in the hot ghetto streets or even if we double our current expenditures for poverty programs. Nothing short of an all-out national effort, with a time schedule, to eradicate the underlying causes of frustration and hopelessness will turn the tide.

The present mood of this nation seems more intent on legislating against riots and uncovering organized conspiracy than on responding to the real issues. The response, or lack of response, of this nation to the *Report of the National Advisory Commission on Civil Disorders*, to the tragic and senseless slaying of Dr. Martin Luther King, Jr., and the almost simultaneous outburst of violence in 130 American cities gives reason to seriously question whether we as a nation are capable of coming to grips with the realities we face. In fact, it is not at all clear that we, as a nation, even understand what is happening to us.

Some have given up all hope of finding a sensible solution—others appear to be on the brink of despair. This sense of near hopelessness and despair is dramatically portrayed on the *empty* front page of the April 29, 1968 issue of *Christianity and Crisis*. Substituting a blank page for what was to have been an editorial comment on the racial crisis, the editors inserted the following comment in the center of the page:

We asked one of our most "engaged" Editorial Board members to address the problem of the looting and burning in the nation that followed the assassination of Dr. Martin Luther King, Jr., with particular reference to the lack of understanding within the white community of its meaning. After two days, he said, "I can't do it. There's nothing to say that we haven't already said before." We have run out of words, and we are running short of hope.*

* Reprinted from CHRISTIANITY AND CRISIS, April 29, 1968; copyright by Christianity and Crisis, Inc., 1968.

The story of racial crisis in America has been told many times by voices from many walks of life. Millions of words have been spoken and written and published in an effort to tell it like it is—yet we do not hear. Or, if we do hear, we are either incapable of understanding or too calloused to care. Even while making the final editorial corrections on this manuscript, we find ourselves asking, why yet another book on a subject that has been covered so many times? There are many intellectual answers which all, in one way or another, say that this volume treats some aspects of the racial crisis in ways that others have not. Whether or not this is so must be left to other scholars to determine. At this moment in our nation's history, the only justification we can give for yet another book is that we must tell the story again and again until America hears, understands, and responds.

L.H.M.
J.K.H.
K.F.S.
J.R.C.

Civil Violence Research Center
Case Western Reserve University
Cleveland, Ohio
February 18, 1969

chapter one

THE LONG HOT SUMMERS:
Prelude to Chaos?

In late 1967, after the nation's fourth 'long hot summer' of racial violence, a major U.S. manufacturer advertised as follows:

The New Bauer Ordinance Armored Police Car will stop 30-06 rifle bullets at point blank range. It has a 360° turret that will mount a machine gun, riot gun, water cannon, flame thrower and grenade launcher. The body is protected by high voltage electricity. The body is designed to protect against Molotov Cocktails and the vehicle carries sufficient water and foaming agents to put out gasoline fires. Can be used to control riots or just to patrol the tough districts. Plenty of room in the back for stretchers or to take in those unruly prisoners. This vehicle was designed by the same people who designed the XM706 (tank) now being used in Viet Nam.[1]

A twisted bit of satire? A cynical jest reassuring that defense technology has domestic applications, or a bitter put-on about private enterprise finally assuming some of the burdens of our nation's social problems? Unfortunately, the advertisement was in deadly earnest. At least two other vehicle manufacturers ran similar ads in police journals. And, while purchasers have requested and been granted anonymity by the manufacturers, nearly a score of these and similar vehicles are now owned by police forces throughout the nation. In addition, stockpiles of riot con-

---

[1] David Burnham, "Nation's Police Arming for Riots," *New York Times,* January 18, 1968. Copyright 1968 by the New York Times Company. Reprinted by permission.

trol weapons—chemical Mace, tear gas guns, hand grenades, riot guns, etc.—are being assembled by safety officials in untold numbers of our urban areas. Police officers and National Guardsmen are undergoing intensified riot-control training. State legislatures and the U.S. Congress are passing stiffer riot-control and gun-control laws. In February, 1968, the Ohio General Assembly passed a law making it virtually impossible for a police officer who shoots a suspected rioter to be prosecuted. (Some critics have termed the law a license to murder.)

It looks very much as if the nation's police and safety officials are in a state of mobilization in preparation for civil war.[2] While their actions may be criticized, they are at least understandable. Several of the nation's urban areas during the last four summers have had the same sights, sounds, and smells one would imagine lingered throughout Dresden after the Allied bombardments. Rubble . . . firebells . . . cries of anguish . . . smoke . . . gunpowder . . . and the stench of death. And, even as in war, there were the troops of occupation: National Guardsmen stationed at every corner, or patrolling the streets in jeeps mounted with fifty caliber machine guns. While rioting had been serious in the summers of 1964, 1965 and 1966, the summer of 1967 was by far the worst. The violence continued, almost without a day's respite, for nearly four months, in one city after another. Depending on the criteria used to identify a riot, anywhere from 75 to 125 American cities felt the pangs of civil violence in 1967. Moreover, numerous investigations indicate that literally scores of incidents which might have become riots were nipped at the bud.

The cities of the nation have become a racial battleground. Advertisements for armored cars for riot control and mobilization as if for war are responses to the summers of violence that preceded and precipitated them. The scream of a siren through the Negro area of any one of our cities triggers the fear and anticipation of days of burning, looting, shooting, and death.

We have become a nation preoccupied with rioting and fearful of further disorder—and probably not without justification. In 1967 alone, at least 84 persons lost their lives in rioting; dozens

[2] For an alarming discussion of this viewpoint see: Gary Wills, *The Second Civil War* (New York: Signet Books, 1968); especially Chapter 1, Battle Plans.

more may have perished in the rubble of burning buildings. Nearly 2,000 injuries to civilians and law officers were reported. Out of fear of being arrested for participating in the civil disorder, hundreds more probably did not make their way into the records of hospitals and emergency care centers. Thus, the figure of 2,000 almost certainly underestimates the number of casualties. The McClellan Senate Subcommittee investigating riots reported 4,289 incidents of arson. Property damage was estimated at $160 million, and estimated economic loss exceeded one-half billion dollars. There were over 16,000 arrests in 1967, and the total during the summers of 1965–1967 approached 30,000.[3]

Response to the outburst of violence has been paradoxical. There can be little doubt but that awareness and concern about the riots has penetrated deep into the consciousness of American society. At the same time, for most Americans this concern is academic. Riots occur in Negro ghettos and most Americans do not live in these ghettos—indeed, most seldom have an opportunity even to get very close to them. Riots occur down *there* in *their* section of the city. Most Americans have not been touched directly by the immediate personal fear and danger of the urban disorders—at least thus far.

Others have not been so lucky. Forty-nine-year-old Fred Williams lived in the Detroit ghetto. He was "one of the clearly innocent victims of the riot, a blameless man doomed to death by an unknown arsonist."[4] His home was threatened by fire from nearby burning stores, and as Williams went to retrieve some clothing, he apparently fell onto fallen electrical wires in the burning alley.

While some were completely innocent, others were sucked into the disorders by the passions of the moment and added to the lists of victims. Twenty-four-year-old William Furr had been stranded in Newark when the rioting prevented his bus back to Montclair from leaving the city. Furr had come to Newark to pick up a $50 unemployment compensation check and to search again for a job.

[3] Data in preceding paragraph from: United States Senate, Hearings Before the Permanent Subcommittee of Investigations of the Committee on Government Operations, *Riots, Civil and Criminal Disorders*, Part I (Washington D. C.: Government Printing Office, 1967).

[4] For an extensive report on the Detroit riot deaths see: "The 43 Who Died," *Detroit Free Press*, September 3, 1967.

Two *Life* magazine reporters documented in extraordinary detail
the sequence of events that prevented Furr from ever returning
home to his mother and grandparents in Montclair.

The reporters came across Furr on Avon Avenue. He and friends
were looting Mack Liquors, loading cases of beer into the trunks
of parked autos. As one of the reporters approached, Furr handed
him a can of beer and said, "Have a beer on me, but if the cops
show up get rid of it and run like hell."[5] A few minutes later, a
police car pulled up in front of the liquor store:

> There had been no warning—it had raced in with its siren silent.
> This was the first sign of police authority on the block in more than
> an hour, except for a young Newark police trainee who had sipped
> beer and watched the looting with me.[6]

The other looters inside the store were trapped. They froze with
their hands above their heads or fell to the floor. Furr was outside
with a six-pack in his hand. He ran. The *Life* reporter describes
what followed:

> He (William Furr) raced past me down Avon. I was barely 30
> feet away from a yellow-helmeted officer with a shotgun pointed
> toward my head.
> 'Get down,' he screamed. I fell hard to the sidewalk just as a
> blast from the weapon exploded over me and the officer shouted an
> order to halt. But apparently Billy kept running behind me. From
> the ground I looked up into the sweating face of the policeman as he
> squinted down the long barrel. I prayed he wouldn't shoot. He pulled
> the trigger.
> Tiny pieces of the spent shell fluttered down on me as blue uniform
> trousers of the Newark Police Department flashed past toward Billy
> lying on the ground. Already people were screaming obscenities from
> the windows and bottles arched from a rooftop. More gunfire cleared
> the windows for a moment, but they quickly filled again.
> 'Call an ambulance,' a policeman yelled back to the car. Up the
> street the officer who had shot Billy stood over him, the shotgun
> resting in the crook of his arm. Billy's blood poured onto the dirty
> sidewalk. Then a girl was beside him sobbing and ignoring the order
> to 'get the hell out of here.'
> 'I'm his girl friend. Help him. Please do something. God, don't let
> him die,' she pleaded.

[5] Dale Wittner, "The Killing of Billy Furr, Caught in the Act of Looting
Beer," *Life*, July 28, 1967, p. 21. Copyright 1967, Time, Inc.
[6] *Ibid.*

William Furr died on the street. A few yards away, another body felled by the same shotgun blast that killed Furr lay bleeding. Joe Bass, Jr., a twelve-year-old Negro was severely wounded in the neck and thigh.

Around his form (Joey's) surged about 50 sobbing men and women, trying to break through the small ring of police. Nearby two other youngsters cried quietly on the curb. The people who wanted to help were clubbed away with rifle and shotgun butts. Their frantic efforts kept the police too busy to help the boy, who we all thought was dying. One Negro appeared to try to snatch the pistol from an officer's holster. He was knocked to the pavement.[7]

Though Bass's wounds were serious, he survived. The *Life* photographer had caught the details of the emotion-packed moments— moments of looting, of police arriving, of Furr running, of police aiming, of Furr dying, of Bass bleeding.

Similar scenes were reported throughout the nation. Streets tattered with litter, crowded with terrified and helpless and defiant Negroes, and swarming with terrified and helpless and defiant policemen and troopers, and with blood flowing from the wounds of both.

In Jackson, Mississippi (May 12–14), thirty law officers and thirteen civilians were injured. In Plainfield, New Jersey (July 16–20), seven law officers and forty-eight civilians. In New York City (July 23–25), thirty-five law officers and ten civilians. And the list goes on and on. Many were injured severely, but the injured in most of these cities lived.

In Detroit, many died. In eight days of rioting, forty-three persons were killed. But not even the number can begin to reflect the tragedy of their deaths. Forty-five-year-old Walter Grzanka was shot by Hamid Audish Yacoub. Yacoub was cruising around his store in the riot area when he spotted Grzanka looting his store. Yacoub shot the unarmed looter without giving him a chance to surrender.

Herman Ector died for walking past the wrong store at the wrong time. The thirty-year-old Army veteran was shot and killed by an unlicensed private watchman (who probably should not have been in the riot area to begin with). Ector was walking with his

[7] *Ibid.*, p. 22.

cousin from his mother's to his aunt's home. Witnesses told police
that Ector objected to the way Waverly Solomon, the unlicensed
guard, was treating suspected looters. Solomon followed the pair
past the store he was supposedly guarding, argued with Ector,
struck him with the butt of his carbine, and then shot him. Ector
was dead by the time he reached the hospital.

Four-year-old Tonia Blanding was shot during a fierce battle
between snipers and National Guardsmen. The Negro child was
killed by bullets believed to have been fired from a guardsman's
machine gun.

After an extensive study of the riot deaths, the *Detroit Free
Press* reported:

A majority of the riot victims need not have died. Their deaths
could have been—and should have been prevented.[8]

One wonders how many more of the nearly 100 deaths recorded
during 1967's rioting fall into the same category.

But the story doesn't begin with the deaths of rioters and law
officers; nor does it even begin with the sirens screeching in the
Negro districts of scores of cities as Molotov Cocktails crashed
through windows and snipers' rifles crackled. The riots did not just
happen. A complex of events, trends, and attitudes with deep roots
in American history and society produced the environment which
allows the violence of the 1960's. These complex underlying conditions must be understood if we are to avert the most tragic
chapter in American history.

The fact of a Negro ghetto, while not widely known or understood by most of white America, is well-established in American
urban history. White America can never fully comprehend the
ghetto's horror or experience its personal degeneration.

But the ghetto is only the most recent form of depravity imposed
upon the Negro. Earlier there was the Jim Crow South's systematic
attempt to destroy the Negro spirit.

Author Richard Wright grew up in that South. The brutality
he describes is incredible. From his earliest years, he recalls violence directed at breaking his spirit, at training him for living
in a world where he would be treated as subhuman. Wright reflects on this molding of an entire race into a people devoid of

[8] *Detroit Free Press, op. cit.*

any sense of self-identity or emotion except hatred and a half-will to survive:

> After I had outlived the shocks of childhood, after the habit of reflection had been born in me, I used to mull over the strange absence of real kindness in Negroes, how unstable was our tenderness, how lacking in genuine passion we were, how void of great hope, how timid our joy, how bare our traditions, how hollow our memories, how lacking we were in those intangible sentiments that bind man to man, and how shallow was even our despair. After I learned other ways of life I used to brood upon the unconscious irony of those who felt that Negroes led so passional an existence! I saw what had been taken for our emotional strength was our negative confusions, our flights, our fears, our frenzy under pressure. Whenever I thought of the essential bleakness of black life in America, I knew that Negroes had never been allowed to catch the full spirit of Western civilization, that they lived somehow in it but not of it. And when I brooded upon the cultural barrenness of black life, I wondered if clean, positive tenderness, love, honor, loyalty, and the capacity to remember were native with man. I asked myself if these human qualities were not fostered, won, struggled and suffered for, preserved in ritual from one generation to another.[9]

A quarter of a century later Claude Brown wrote about growing up in a northern ghetto. His *Manchild in the Promised Land* tells of violence and depravity worthy of the Jim Crow South. He tells of raising expectations which are shattered by the stark realization that nothing has really changed:

> I want to talk about the first Northern urban generation of Negroes. I want to talk about the experiences of a misplaced generation, of a misplaced people in an extremely complex, confused society. This is a story of their searching, their dreams, their sorrows, their small and futile rebellions, and their endless battle to establish their own place in America's greatest metropolis—and in America itself.
> The characters are sons and daughters of former Southern share-croppers. These were the poorest people of the South, who poured into New York City during the decade following the Great Depression. These migrants were told that unlimited opportunities for prosperity existed in New York and that there was no "color problem" there. They were told that Negroes lived in houses with bathrooms, electricity, running water, and indoor toilets. To them, this was the "promised land" that Mammy had been singing about in the cotton fields for many years.

---

[9] Richard Wright, *Black Boy: A Record of Childhood and Youth* (New York: Harper & Row, Publishers, 1966), p. 45.

Going to New York was good-bye to the cotton fields, good-bye to
"Massa Charlie," good-bye to the chain gang, and, most of all, good-
bye to those sunup-to-sundown working hours. One no longer had to
wait to get to heaven to lay his burden down; burdens could be laid
down in New York.

So they came, from all parts of the South, like all the black
chillun o' God following the sound of Gabriel's horn on that long-
overdue Judgment Day. The Georgians came as soon as they were
able to pick train fare off the peach trees. They came from South
Carolina where the cotton stalks were bare. The North Carolinians
came with tobacco tar beneath their fingernails.

They felt as the Pilgrims must have felt when they were coming
to America. But these descendants of Ham must have been twice as
happy as the Pilgrims, because they had been catching twice the hell.
Even while planning the trip, they sang spirituals as "Jesus Take My
Hand" and "I'm On My Way" and chanted, "Hallelujah, I'm on my
way to the promised land!"

It seems that Cousin Willie, in his lying haste, had neglected to tell
the folks down home about one of the most important aspects of the
promised land: it was a slum ghetto. There was a tremendous difference in the way life was lived up North. There were too many people
full of hate and bitterness crowded into a dirty, stinky, uncared-for
closet-size section of a great city.

Before the soreness of the cotton fields had left Mama's back, her
knees were getting sore from scrubbing "Goldberg's" floor. Nevertheless, she was better off; she had gone from the fire into the frying pan.

The children of these disillusioned colored pioneers inherited the
total lot of their parents—the disappointments, the anger. To add to
their misery, they had little hope of deliverance. For where does one
run to when he's already in the promised land?[10]

From childhood, then, in North and South, the brief glimpses
into the subworld imposed upon the Negro show more than mere
physical deprivation. They show the more devastating dimension
of the Negro's condition in America—the psychological destruction
of the Negro as a self-respecting human being. Both Wright and
Brown have, to some extent, escaped the worst evils of the Negro
condition. But for the large majority of black Americans, the
suppression continues.

The Civil Rights movement in America has attempted to allevi-
ate this oppression. But, more than simply an attempt to right
centuries of wrongs, the movement is a complex and subtle mix

[10] Claude Brown, *Manchild in the Promised Land* (New York: The
Macmillan Company, 1965), pp. 7–8.

of men and their goals, their faiths, their methods, and dreams. It is the evangelical mission and martyrdom of a Martin Luther King, Jr., the humor and fervent commitment of a Dick Gregory, the sacrifice of a Medgar Evers, the slaughter of a Malcom X, and even the hatred of a Stokely Carmichael or a Rap Brown.

By 1962 Dick Gregory had 'made it big' as an entertainer. Yet he felt that his personal success was insufficient, that he had a commitment to his race. While participating in the opening of San Francisco's *hungry i*, Gregory spoke with Medgar Evers—who was then leading the demonstrations in Jackson, Mississippi. Evers asked Gregory to join in the marches. Like many of the minority of Negroes who have made it, Gregory responded to the call, despite his apprehensions:

It was that last night in San Francisco, a Saturday night, that I first felt death. Just a funny little feeling in my stomach, a sixth sense that said someone was going to die. I called my lawyer to make sure my will was in order. Then I flew to Chicago to talk to Lil. If I was killed in Jackson, I didn't want my children raised with hate.

She sat on the couch, her eyes wide and tearful, and I told her what I wanted my children to hear. Just tell them that Daddy was doing right, Lil, tell them it takes a strong soldier to fight when he's outnumbered and the other side has all the dogs, all the fire hoses, all the prods. Don't let them come up with hate, Lil; just show them the beauty in what their Daddy was doing.

I went into the bedroom and I kissed Michele and Lynne, and I kissed Richard Claxton Gregory Junior. He was two and a half months old, and I hadn't had time to know him.[11]

Gregory left for Jackson. Upon arriving, Evers informed him that his infant son, Richard, Jr., had died of overnight pneumonia. Gregory rushed back to his home in Chicago. In his moving account in *Nigger*, Gregory describes the personal anguish he and his family underwent over the death of his son, and over the realization that had the baby not died Gregory himself might have been killed in Mississippi: Evers was shot and killed.

Gregory's commitment was essentially to the same nonviolent principles put forth by the Reverend King. Others such as Malcolm X stood at their platforms and shouted:

---

[11] This story is drawn from pp. 181–189 of *Nigger: An Autobiography* by Dick Gregory with Robert Lipsyte (New York: Pocket Books, Inc., 1965). Reprinted by permission of the publisher, E. P. Dutton & Co., Inc.

America is the last stronghold of white supremacy. The Black Revolution, which is international in nature and scope, is sweeping down upon America like a raging forest fire. It is only a matter of time before America herself will be engulfed by these black flames, these black firebrands.[12]

Though Malcolm X was assassinated, others have taken the lead in advocating violence. Stokely Carmichael has traveled abroad and sent back press releases—datelined Havana or Hanoi—condemning white America. H. Rap Brown has stood in the streets of Cambridge, Maryland, and shouted to Negroes who in a few short hours were rioting in the streets:

Brothers, you've got to get some guns. I don't care if its B-B guns with poisoned B-Bs. He's done declared war on black people. He don't mind killing them. It might be your son he kills next. Or it might be your daughter. Or it might be you. So, wherever you go, brother, take some of them with you. That's what you do, brother. An eye for an eye; a tooth for a tooth. Tit for tat, brother, that's the only kind of war the man knows. That's the only thing he recognizes. Ain't no need in the world for me to come to Cambridge and I see all them stores sitting up there and all them honkies owns them. You got to own some of them stores. I don't care if you have to burn him down and run him out. You's better take over them stores. The streets are yours, Take 'em. They gave you the streets a long time ago; before they gave you houses. They gave you the streets. So, we own the streets. Take 'em. You've got to take 'em. They ain't going to give them to you.[13]

It is hard to talk about the civil rights movement, for it is a kaleidoscope of a thousand moods and faces. It is a highly personal thing. But it is also a cultural phenomenon in which all of us, black and white, no matter how personally removed we may feel, are participating and are being affected. What we do not do —perhaps even more than what we do, consciously and unconsciously—is molding the direction of this movement.

The movement has had some notable successes. On the morning of November 8, 1967 in Cleveland, Ohio, a crowd was gathered

[12] Malcolm X, "God's Judgement of White America," a speech to a public rally at Manhattan Center, December 1, 1963; reprinted in *Evergreen*, December, 1967.

[13] H. Rap Brown, address at Cambridge, Maryland, on July 24, 1967, reprinted in *Anti-Riot Bill—1967*, Hearings before the United States Senate, Committee on the Judiciary, 90th Congress, First Session (Washington, D. C.: Government Printing Office, 1967).

at one of two opposing downtown campaign headquarters to hear the results of the mayoral election. At 3:30 A.M., the Board of Elections announced that Carl Stokes, a Negro, was mayor. A middle-aged Negro smiled and said, "Shit, man, we got us a mayor." A young Negro shouted, "We don't gotta burn tonight." And hundreds of young Negroes danced in the streets until dawn —the same streets where many of them had rioted in 1966.

Civil rights legislation is being passed, Negroes are moving into jobs that Negroes have never before occupied, into homes in suburbs that have heretofore been for whites only.

Ask most white Americans, and they can rattle off seemingly endless examples of progress. But ask most Negroes in the ghetto and you get a different picture.

The truth of the matter is that the civil rights movement is not going well. It is on the verge of total collapse. And standing in the corridors are the militants who are preparing for the second civil war.

In spite of all the successes we can point to, all of the activity of the past fifteen years has not significantly altered the life chances of the large majority of black Americans. In fact, a large proportion of Negroes are worse off today than they were before the civil rights movement began.

This is hard for white America to grasp, but it is true. It is even harder for white America to understand that the economic and psychological disabilities of the masses of Negroes are not of their own making. As a nation, we believe that men are the masters of their own fate. Perhaps, most of us can acknowledge, this has not always been the case for the Negro. But discrimination has been outlawed. The Negro has joined a nation of rugged individualists in the struggle for the rewards of a rich and thriving economic system. He could make it if he were willing to take advantage of the opportunities that are now available to him. He could solve his own problems if he were not so irresponsible and carefree about life. And we can all point to Negroes who have or who are making it, so we know it must be true.

But we seem incapable of understanding that our laws and our ideologies, which would like to believe that all men are free, do not in fact make this true. Perhaps the most blatant forms of prejudice and discrimination are disappearing. But we remain largely blind and insensitive to the hundreds of ways in which subtle forms of prejudice and discrimination block the Negro's movement into the mainstream of American life.

Nor do we seem able to understand that laws and even dramatic changes in attitudes do not change history. The atrocities of the past continue to haunt the Negro. Individuals may escape this history, just as a boy from a log cabin escaped his lowly origins and rose to the presidency of this nation. But these are rare cases. The large majority of Negroes cannot become full participants in our society until we have removed the shackles of history.

Negroes have had a taste of freedom. It is no longer ours to withhold or make conditional. If we do not understand the fullest implications of what this means, then it is doubtful that any of us shall be free much longer.

Those who try to separate the riots of the past five summers from the nonviolent marches of the preceding summers are either naive or dishonest. But this is not to say that the nonviolent civil disobedience of the Southern Christian Leadership Conference has *caused* the riots. Both are logical and predictable developments in the struggle of a suppressed people to free themselves. Neither violence nor nonviolence can be understood outside this historical process.

This book is an attempt to interpret the violence of the past five summers from this historical perspective. It is an attempt to analyze the underlying conditions which have produced a nation torn internally and on the verge of a race war, and very possibly on the brink of self-destruction.

chapter two

THE GROWING CRISIS
IN BLACK AND WHITE
(1954–1965)

1954—THE SUPREME COURT AND THE SCHOOLS

On May 17, 1954, the U. S. Supreme Court handed down what most Americans immediately—and correctly—recognized as a decision of monumental significance. The case was *Brown v. Topeka Board of Education*.[1] The issue was a previous Supreme Court ruling—in 1896—in the case of *Plessy v. Ferguson*.[2] At stake was the relevance of the precedent established in the Plessy case to school segregation of Kansas Negroes.

The precedent of the Plessy decision was deceptively simple. It established the constitutionality of providing separate facilities for Negroes as long as they were comparable to similar facilities provided for whites. In the Brown case, the Court's rationale in striking down the separate but equal precedent would likewise be simple: the fact of separation precluded the fact of equality. Or, in the words of Chief Justice Earl Warren:

We conclude that in the field of public education the doctrine of "separate but equal" has no place. Separate education facilities are inherently unequal. Therefore, we hold that the plaintiffs and others similarly situated for whom the actions have been brought are, by

[1] *Brown v. Board of Education of Topeka, Kansas*, 347 U.S. 483.
[2] *Plessy v. Ferguson*, 163 U.S. 537.

13

reason of the segregation complained of, deprived of the equal protection of the laws guaranteed by the Fourteenth Amendment.[3]

Realizing the broad implications of its action and, particularly, the obstacles involved in the implementation of the decree, the Court postponed its order to put into effect the desegregation ruling for one year. On May 31, 1955, the order was given. School segregation, in the form of laws based on the separate but equal doctrine, had been crushed. Serious doubt was cast on the constitutionality of any laws based on the reasoning of the *Plessy v. Ferguson* case.

The Supreme Court decision was the beginning of a path which would prove to be long, complex, and sometimes hazardous. Along it were the sit-ins, the boycotts, the forcible desegregation of public schools and universities, the demonstrations and protest marches, the confrontation of legislators and their attempts to deal with the problem, and finally the emergence of new moods of militancy.

The most significant aspect of this initial victory of the civil rights movement was the manner in which it was achieved, because this was to be the tone for the decade to come. The tone was nonviolent protest; the route was an appeal to legal and rational factors.

The campaign began in 1950. Thurgood Marshall, chief counsel for the National Association for the Advancement of Colored People, leveled the attack at the American legal system. To win, he mustered not only the best legal minds available, but also the findings of sociologists, psychologists, and educators—findings which would shatter the myth that separate could be equal.

For a decade of struggle, the legal approach to win the equality of the Negro was the dominant theme of the civil rights effort. Marshall became one of many Negro leaders who urged his people to achieve significant progress by impressing the American conscience with the deprivation of the Negro in America and by the concurrent use of legal means. *De jure* recognition seemed assured. But *de facto* gains were still required. A theme had been established. Progress could be made. The nonviolent, legal approach was working.

[3] Chief Justice Earl Warren in the majority opinion to *Brown v. Board of Education of Topeka, Kansas.*

1955—MARTIN LUTHER KING AND THE BUSES

On December 1, 1955, Mrs. Rosa Parks, a Negro seamstress, boarded the Cleveland Avenue bus in downtown Montgomery, Alabama. She sat in the Negro section, but in the first seat behind the section reserved for whites. Soon after, the bus operator ordered her, along with three other Negro passengers, to move back in order to make room for whites boarding the bus. The three others moved. Mrs. Parks did not. Her refusal to abide by the operator's order and her subsequent arrest set into motion a chain of events that moved the Negro's struggle for equality from the courts to the streets—and to the masses who populated the streets. Equally important, the chain of events which followed established the prominence of a young Negro minister, Martin Luther King Jr., whose philosophy and approach seemed to assure that the struggle's theme would remain that of reason and non-violence.

Local Negro leaders called a one-day boycott of the city's buses on December 5 to protest the arrest. The action was prompted by the concern of a Pullman porter, Ed Nixon, who posted bail for Mrs. Parks and made her plight known to members of the Negro community. The leaders of the Negro community formed the Montgomery Improvement Association. The Reverend Martin Luther King, newly appointed pastor of the Dexter Avenue Baptist Church, was selected to lead the one-day protest against segregated bus facilities.

Three hundred and eighty-five days later the protest ended—but not until the Supreme Court ordered an end to segregated seating on public buses.

During the course of the struggle, Martin Luther King and his philosophy matured. The Montgomery Bus Boycott and King's subsequent book on the protest, *Stride Toward Freedom*, established the young minister as the leader of the emerging civil rights movement. His appeal spread throughout the Negro populace and even captured the imagination of many members of the white community.

While the boycott was in progress, King had faced a critical personal decision: should he place himself in a position of prominence in the civil rights struggle? He had continuously received threats during the course of the protest. One night, he was roused from his bed by a phone call. The embittered anonymous voice from the other end of the line threatened: "Listen, nigger, we've taken all we want from you; before next week you'll be sorry you ever came to Montgomery."[4]

Deeply disturbed, King could not return to sleep. The decision had to be made. Could he continue and carry through what he had begun in Montgomery? Did he have the strength and courage? Did he have justification? In a moving account, King himself describes how he faced his personal crisis:

I got out of bed and began to walk the floor. Finally, I went to the kitchen and heated a pot of coffee. I was ready to give up. With my cup of coffee sitting untouched before me I tried to think of a way to move out of the picture without appearing a coward. In this state of exhaustion, when my courage had all but gone, I decided to take my problem to God. With my head in my hands, I bowed over the kitchen table and prayed aloud. The words I spoke to God that midnight are still vivid in my memory. "I am here taking a stand for what I believe is right. But now I am afraid. The people are looking to me for leadership, and if I stand before them without strength and courage, they too will falter. I am at the end of my powers. I have nothing left. I've come to the point where I can't face it alone."

At that moment I experienced the presence of the Divine as I had never experienced Him before. It seemed as though I could hear the quiet assurance of an inner voice saying: "Stand up for righteousness, stand up for truth; and God will be at your side forever." Almost at once my fears began to go. My uncertainty disappeared. I was ready to face anything.[5]

Martin Luther King had made his decision. The civil rights movement had a leader. For almost the next decade, his thinking and direction were to guide the Negro in his quest for equality. The world would not again be the same.

1957—THE CONGRESS AND THE SPIRIT

On September 9, 1957, President Eisenhower signed into law the first civil rights bill passed since Reconstruction. In Dr. King's

---

[4] Martin Luther King, *Stride Toward Freedom: The Montgomery Story* (New York: Harper & Row, Publishers; Perennial Library Edition, 1964), pp. 114–115.
[5] *Ibid.*

term, the *zeitgeist* or spirit of the time had finally reached the halls of Congress. With this occurrence, another decision-making body of the nation became involved in pressing forward the Negro's struggle for equality.

The legislation, however, had not come without long debate and considerable controversy. Moreover, it was not the long hoped-for benchmark which would establish the new legal framework for interracial relations throughout the country. Rather, it was— as is all but the most innocuous legislation—a compromise. Civil rights groups later referred to it as "the minimum meaningful bill they could accept."[6]

The law itself had four major aspects, providing for:

the establishment of a special Civil Rights Division within the Department of Justice;

the creation of a Federal Civil Rights Commission with power of subpoena to study the status of civil rights in the nation and to make recommendations for legislation;

the authorization of the Justice Department to intervene, in the name of the U.S., on behalf of individuals whose civil rights were threatened or violated; and

the authorization of Federal intervention against threats or violations against the right to vote.[7]

The legislation did not redefine any rights, nor propose any new way of living. Rather, it set up mechanisms—mechanisms to investigate the need for new legislation and to enforce existing laws. At last, the years of congressional apathy since Reconstruction had come to an end.

1957—ORVAL AND IKE

At Little Rock's all-white Central High School, ten Negro children had registered for the fall term, beginning on September 4, 1957. Their right to attend classes at Central had been guaranteed by the Supreme Court in 1954. But neither the court justices nor the children had reckoned on Orval Faubus.

Faubus, governor of Arkansas, ordered the state's National Guardsmen to put Central off limits to Negroes. Nine of the ten

---

[6] Lynne Ianniello (editor), *Milestones Along the March* (New York: Frederick A. Praeger, 1965), p. 57.

[7] *Ibid.*, pp. 57–58.

registered students attempted to enter the school on opening day. The guardsmen blocked their passage. Two weeks later, on September 20, a federal court issued an order calling for removal of the National Guard and admission of the Negroes to classes.

The guardsmen were withdrawn on September 22. In their stead, nearly a thousand white supremacists appeared the next day around Central High. Their proclaimed goal: to keep the Negroes from entering at all costs.

Shortly before 9:00 A.M., the appearance of four Negro newsmen diverted the attention of the mob. The nine children walked into Central High untouched—and almost without notice—while the mob chased and beat the newsmen. However, the threat of additional mob violence forced the Little Rock mayor and school superintendent to withdraw the students from school. As a heavy police guard escorted them away, the three-hour integration of the Little Rock school system ended, at least temporarily.

That evening, President Eisenhower signed a proclamation ordering "all persons" obstructing the court-ordered integration in Little Rock "to cease and desist therefrom and to disperse forthwith."

Mobs gathered around Central High the next morning in defiance of the presidential proclamation. At 12:22 P.M., the President issued an executive order authorizing the Secretary of Defense to use all military forces necessary to uphold the Little Rock court order. Two hours later, Secretary of Defense Charles Wilson federalized the Arkansas National Guard and dispatched a thousand paratroopers from Fort Campbell, Kentucky, to take up positions outside the school. Two civilians suffered minor injuries and seven were arrested in scuffles with the troops. General Edwin Walker, in command of the federalized guardsmen and the paratroopers, addressed the white student body before the Negroes entered the school. Meanwhile his troops enforced a ban on mob gatherings around the school. Seven hundred and fifty of the white students, out of two thousand enrolled, were not present to hear Walker. A few white students left school after the Negroes arrived, but no disorders were reported among the students inside the school.

The paratroopers remained in Little Rock until May 8, 1958. The same day the paratroopers departed, the President announced that the federalized guardsmen would leave Central High at the start of the summer recess on May 29. Eisenhower had regretted his own decision to deploy armed force against the citizens of Little Rock. He felt he had been coerced. He was right. Principles and circumstances had required him to act, and he chose the only viable option.

1960—STUDENTS AND SIT-INS

On February 1, 1960, four freshmen from the all-Negro Agricultural and Technical College in Greensboro, North Carolina, entered a Woolworth's Drug Store. They made some purchases, sat at the lunch counter, and placed their orders. When refused service, the four students remained in their seats until the store closed. The relatively mild and minor incident grew into a veritable maelstrom, triggering a major series of similar incidents by other Negro students at segregated lunch counters in other cities. Eventually the Negro students were joined by sympathetic white students. Organizers from groups such as the Congress of Racial Equality and the Southern Christian Leadership Conference began conducting workshops in nonviolent resistance for the youthful protesters. The students' blatant disregard for the traditional mores of Southern society shocked much of white America—in both the North and the South. But the students were not to be denied. As one observer reflected:

Young Negroes in the South had forgotten their "proper place," and as the movement spread it destroyed the established etiquette and mythology of Southern race relations.[8]

As in earlier protests, nonviolence was used to assert the equal rights of the Negro. The often violent reaction of the white community to the sit-ins aided in appealing to the consciousness and conscience of an America which had failed to grant the Negro those rights. As with the bus boycott, the sit-ins destroyed much of the mythology and probed for the realization of the meaning of the Court's action in 1954. 'Separate but equal,' tested and defeated in the courts, was now being tested in the streets. The movement had again gone from the lawyers to the masses.

As it did, hundreds of lunch counters across the South began

---

[8] Gilbert Osofsky (editor), *The Burden of Race* (New York: Harper & Row, Publishers, Inc., 1967), pp. 526–527.

to serve Negroes. When sit-ins failed to bend a recalcitrant owner or community, boycotting and selective buying were used to bring effective economic pressure upon the noncompliants.

Far from simple participation in a fad, many of the students involved in the sit-ins saw the true relevance of their actions in the struggle to move from *de jure* recognition of rights to *de facto* equality. The vast majority had also truly incorporated the nonviolent spirit preached and practiced by Dr. King and his followers.

The understanding and determination of many of these students is best expressed in their own words. Patricia Stephens, a student at Florida A & M, wrote these words from her jail cell in Leon County, Florida. She had been held there after her arrest for participation in a sit-in.

My sister Priscilla and I, five other A & M students and one high school student are serving 60-day sentences for our participation in the sit-ins. We could be out on appeal but we all strongly believe that Martin Luther King was right when he said: "We've got to fill the jails in order to win our equal rights." Priscilla and I both explained this to our parents when they visited us the other day. Priscilla is supposed to be on a special diet and mother was worried about her. We made it clear that we want to serve-out our full time.[9]

This then was the strategy of the campaign. To demand a right to be served. When refused, sit in. If arrested and jailed, serve the sentence and fill the jails. Nonviolent resistance was the heart of the struggle. And the struggle gained attention, caused trouble, stirred serious thought, and produced some results.

1961—BULL CONNOR AND MOTHER'S DAY

By 1960, the Supreme Court had outlawed all segregation in interstate transportation. The court's rulings were all-inclusive, ranging from segregation in the seating of passengers to segregation in any of the facilities (depots, terminals, lunch counters, restrooms) associated with interstate transport.

In 1961, the leaders of the Congress of Racial Equality decided

---

[9] Patricia Stephens, "Tallahassee: Through Jail to Freedom," in Osofsky, *op. cit.*, p. 527.

to test these rulings. CORE assembled a group of Negroes in Washington, D. C. Their itinerary took them through the heart of the deep South on their way to New Orleans. The test was to be nonviolent.

The riders bought tickets on two different bus lines and rode with the regular passengers. Until they reached Danville, Virginia, the Negroes were served almost without question at each stop the bus made. Even at Danville, they were served after a brief discussion with the manager of the establishment.

The remainder of the trip was not so peaceful.

Incidents of refusal of service became more numerous as the riders traveled farther South. Along the way, some of the riders were arrested for seeking service. The arrested were, however, subsequently released. The local police could not find grounds for bringing charges against them in light of the recent Supreme Court rulings.

Those not temporarily detained by police along the way continued their journey and met their most belligerent resistance in Anniston and Birmingham, Alabama. The buses were scheduled to pass through these cities on May 14, Mother's Day. As James Peck, one of the participants in the freedom ride, recalls:

> The most nightmarish day of our freedom ride was Sunday, May 14, Mother's Day. I identify the date with Mother's Day because when police chief Connor was asked why there was not a single policeman at the Birmingham Trailways terminal to avert mob violence, he explained that since it was Mother's Day, most of the police were off-duty visiting their mothers. That there was going to be a mob to meet us had been well known around Birmingham for several days. Reverend Fred Shuttlesworth told me so when I phoned to give him the scheduled arrival times of our two buses.[10]

When the first bus pulled into Anniston, an angry mob armed with iron bars immediately surrounded it. The mob vented its anger on the bus, denting its sides and breaking windows. When police arrived, the bus managed to depart, but the mob pursued in cars. Just outside Anniston, a flat tire forced the bus to stop at a gas station. Within minutes, the mob again attacked the bus.

[10] James Peck, "Freedom Ride—Washington to New Orleans," in Alan Westin (editor), *Freedom Now!* (New York: Basic Books, Inc., 1964), pp. 245–246.

A bomb hurled through the broken rear window filled the bus with smoke. All the passengers managed to escape the vehicle before it burst into flames. At that point, the local police—bystanders for most of the incident—moved into the crowd, fired a few shòts, and dispersed the mob.

When the second bus arrived in Anniston, the freedom riders learned of what had happened ahead of them and decided to discontinue the trip. Before they could depart, however, a group of hoodlums boarded the bus and began fighting with the freedom riders, forcing them to the seats usually reserved for Negroes. When the bus departed for Birmingham, whites rode in front, the middle seats were empty, and Negroes rode in the rear.

A waiting mob greeted the bus upon arrival in Birmingham. When the freedom riders disembarked, they were attacked and many beaten severely. The freedom ride was at an end. The participants then boarded a plane to New Orleans, where a mass rally had been planned to mark the end of the freedom ride and the May 17th anniversary of the Supreme Court's historic 1954 decision on desegregation.

The indecisive result of this first test of desegregation of interstate transportation facilities led to more tests. Subsequent groups of Negroes, along with sympathetic whites, participated in freedom rides throughout the South. The Freedom Riders Coordinating Committee was formed by the Congress of Racial Equality, the Southern Christian Leadership Conference, the Student Nonviolent Coordinating Committee, and the Nashville Student Movement to direct the activities of over 1,000 volunteers. In the subsequent tests, the volunteers met violence and arrest with regularity.

C. Eric Lincoln, in his survey of the Negro protest movement, writes:

> Violence and tension in Alabama, particularly in the capital city of Montgomery, reached the point that six hundred Federal marshals were sent into that city to protect the riders and restore order. In Mississippi, the buses carrying the Freedom Riders were escorted to Jackson under heavy guard, whereupon more than three hundred riders, including at least fifteen priests, were arrested and jailed.[11]

[11] C. Eric Lincoln, "The American Protest Movement for Negro Rights," in John P. Davis (editor), *The American Negro Reference Book* (Englewood Cliffs, New Jersey: Prentice-Hall, Inc., 1966), p. 474.

Subsequent tests proved more effective than the initial one. Ultimately 120 interstate bus terminals were desegregated through the efforts of the freedom riders. On September 23, 1961, the Interstate Commerce Commission ruled that passengers on interstate carriers should be seated without regard to race and that such carriers could not operate segregated terminals. The Supreme Court's rulings on transportation had been translated into an administrative order designed to implement the Court's decision. However, the decision and the gains had not come until the struggle for Negro rights passed from the lawyers and their days in court to the masses and their protests in the streets.

Masses engaged in nonviolent protest seemed to have won their point with the majority of the society. Unfortunately, the nonviolent approach had not meant that violence would be absent, despite the fact that the freedom riders themselves did not encourage or respond violently to threats and attacks. Violence could not remain an irrelevant issue in the continuing struggle to gain *de facto* equality. It appeared again.

1962—MEREDITH AND OL' MISS

On February 1, 1961, Negro James H. Meredith applied for admission to the all-white University of Mississippi. Denied entrance, allegedly on the basis of his color, Meredith filed suit in a U.S. district court, asking the court to order his admission. After a series of lower court decisions, the case reached the Supreme Court. There Justice Hugo Black ordered that the decision of one of the lower courts, the U.S. Court of Appeals for the Fifth Circuit, should stand. That court had ruled that Meredith had indeed been denied admission on the basis of his color. The Supreme Court order was signed only by Justice Black. Though there was no formal hearing before the Court, Black indicated that he had consulted with his fellow justices before acting.

Three days later, on September 13, 1962, Mississippi Governor Ross R. Barnett declared that he would go to jail before admitting a Negro to the state university. Barnett invoked the doctrine of interposition, which holds that a state may interpose its power to protect its citizens against illegal acts on the part of the federal government.

Meredith attempted to enroll at Ol' Miss on September 20th and again on the 25th. Each time Barnett said no. Meredith's third attempt, on the 26th, was met by a show of armed force, in the person of Barnett backed by 400 police officers. In response, the federal government entered the conflict, sending hundreds of federal marshals to Oxford.

Meredith's fourth try came on the 27th. He approached the university accompanied by a convoy of U.S. marshals. The campus was ringed by hundreds of highway patrolmen, sheriffs, deputies, and local police officers. Barnett's forces were armed with gas masks, clubs, helmets, and trained dogs. Their firearms, though not worn, were within easy reach. Nearly 1,000 students and other onlookers watched Meredith and his convoy turned back again.

Meanwhile, Attorney General Robert F. Kennedy was pressing court action against Barnett. On September 25, an appellate court ordered the governor to appear in New Orleans on September 28 or face contempt charges. Barnett failed to appear. The court tried him *in absentia*, found him guilty of civil contempt, and ordered him to admit Meredith by October 2 or face arrest and a fine of $10,000 for each day of delay.

The federal government was winning in the courts while the recalcitrant Barnett was winning on the campus. Citizens of his own and other Southern states rallied to his side. In order for Meredith to attend classes at the university, more than court orders were needed.

President John F. Kennedy responded. On September 29, hundreds of U.S. marshals converged on Oxford, federal troops were alerted for action, and the Mississippi National Guard was federalized.

Violence erupted the next day as Meredith was escorted onto the campus by the marshals. When order was finally restored near dawn the next morning, some 16,000 federal troops had been called to the scene and the town of Oxford was virtually under martial law. Two had died and many more were injured.

Six weeks later, five hundred armed troops and fifteen U.S. marshals were still stationed in Oxford to protect Meredith and to maintain order. At a cost of millions of dollars to the federal and state governments, James Meredith had 'integrated' the University of Mississippi, 19 months after he had first applied for admission.

1963—OPERATION C AND BIRMINGHAM

The infamy attached to Birmingham as a result of the freedom rides was soon overshadowed. In its place, a new notoriety, no more complimentary to the city, emerged out of the protests held during the spring of 1963.

Though the largest industrial center in the South, Birmingham was typical of the many southern cities in which racial hatred abounds. The 40 per cent of the population which was black lived in conditions of deprivation as severe as any in the nation. In his description of the city in 1963, Dr. King hinted at the patterns of suppression that permeated it:

It was a community in which human rights had been trampled for so long that fear and oppression were as thick in its atmosphere as the smog from its factories ...[12]

If you had visited Birmingham before the third of April in the one-hundredth-anniversary year of the Negro's emancipation, you might have come to a startling conclusion. You might have concluded that here was a city which had been trapped for decades in a Rip Van Winkle slumber; a city whose fathers had apparently never heard of Abraham Lincoln, Thomas Jefferson, the Bill of Rights, the Preamble to the Constitution, the Thirteenth, Fourteenth, and Fifteenth Amendments, or the 1954 decision of the United States Supreme Court outlawing segregation in the public schools.[13]

In response to this, the Negro leaders in Birmingham, the Southern Christian Leadership Conference, and Dr. King began planning Operation C in the fall of 1962. It was envisaged by its planners as a major nonviolent protest against the suppression of the Negro in Birmingham. The C stood for confrontation. The target was the Birmingham business community:

We concluded that in hard-core communities a more effective battle could be waged if it was concentrated against one aspect of the evil and intricate system of segregation. We decided, therefore, to center the Birmingham struggle on the business community, for we knew

[12] Martin Luther King, Jr., *Why We Can't Wait*, p. 45. Copyright 1964 by Martin Luther King, Jr. Reprinted by permission of Harper and Row, Publishers.

[13] *Ibid.*, p. 47.

that the Negro population had sufficient buying power so that its withdrawal could make the difference between profit and loss for many
businesses.[14]

The strategy of Operation C was designed to bring maximum
pressure on Birmingham merchants by cutting into their profits
during the year's second largest shopping period, the Easter season.

To insure a successful confrontation, the planners of Operation C
drew plans for their organization carefully. Downtown Birmingham was studied, primary and secondary targets were chosen,
and a training school in nonviolence was established.

The goals of Operation C were four:

the desegregation of lunch counters, restrooms, fitting rooms, and
    drinking fountains in variety and department stores;
the upgrading and hiring of Negroes on a nondiscriminatory basis
    throughout the business and industrial community of Birmingham;
the dropping of all charges against jailed demonstrators; and
the creation of a biracial committee to work out a timetable for de-
    segregation of other areas of Birmingham life.[15]

The launching of Operation C presented a dilemma. King felt
that the demonstrations should begin several weeks before the
Easter season in order to maximize the mobilization of support
from the Negro community. But this proved strategically unwise.
Birmingham faced a mayoralty election on March 5 and Bull
Connor was a candidate. While the other two leading contenders
were segregationists, they were considered moderates when compared to Connor. The S.C.L.C. leadership feared that a major
civil rights thrust in the midst of the mayoralty campaign would
give Connor an advantage among white segregationists who would
see him as the only candidate capable of holding the line against
Negro demands. Thus, Operation C was postponed until after the
election.

But March 5 did not prove to be decisive. No candidate received
a majority of the votes, forcing a run-off between Connor and
Albert Boutwell. The new election was scheduled for April 2, just
twelve days before Easter. Reluctantly, Operation C was again
postponed.

As the polls were closing on April 2, Dr. King flew to Birming-

[14] *Ibid.*, p. 54.
[15] *Ibid.*, pp. 102–103.

ham to begin the confrontation. On Wednesday, April 3, volunteers went in groups of eight to sit-in at lunch counters in the
downtown drug and department stores. By Friday, 35 volunteers
had been arrested and the lunch counters in downtown Birmingham had been closed down.

On Saturday, a group of 125 assembled at the Sixteenth Street
Baptist Church to march on City Hall. They were met by Bull
Connor's officers and 42 were arrested. Palm Sunday saw almost
100 arrested in another march.

The campaign was gaining momentum and support from the
Negro community. Holy Week saw a variety of tactics employed:
kneel-ins, sit-ins, rallies and marches. But the most important
weapon of the confrontation was the boycott of downtown business
establishments. King reported that a careful check a few days
before Easter counted less than 20 Negroes patronizing downtown
businesses.[16]

On April 10, the city of Birmingham secured a court injunction forbidding further demonstrations and marches until such
time as the courts could determine their legality.

Two days later, the Birmingham confrontation and the civil
rights movement in America took on a new dimension. For the
first time, Dr. King and his followers disobeyed a court order.
Dr. King tells why:

We did not take this radical step without prolonged and prayerful
consideration ... When the Supreme Court decision on school desegregation was handed down, leading segregationists vowed to thwart
it by invoking 'a century of litigation.' There was more significance
to this threat than many Americans imagined. The injunction method
has now become the leading instrument of the South to block the
direct-action civil-rights drive ... We decided, therefore, knowing well
what the consequences would be and prepared to accept them, that
we had no choice but to violate such an injunction ... I announced
our plan to the press, pointing out that we were not anarchists advocating lawlessness, but that it was obvious to us that the courts of
Alabama had misused the judicial process in order to perpetuate
injustice and segregation. Consequently, we could not, in good conscience, obey their findings.[17]

---

[16] *Ibid.*, p. 69. It seems to us unlikely that so few Negroes patronized
downtown business establishments in a full day, but it is clear that the
boycott was effective.

[17] *Ibid.*, pp. 70–71.

King, himself, led the march on Good Friday which disobeyed the court injunction and was arrested. The days that followed were critical. The city notified the bondsman who had been furnishing bail that his funds were inadequate and that he would have to suspend his operation. S.C.L.C.'s funds for bail bond were exhausted. With King and Ralph Abernathy in jail, the collapse of the confrontation seemed apparent. During these critical days, Harry Belafonte raised $50,000 for bail bonds.

On April 20, King and Abernathy accepted bond and emerged from imprisonment with a renewed determination to win the confrontation. The new strategy, inspired by James Bevel, was to fill the jails. On May 2, more than 1,000 students marched and were arrested. A few days later, more than 2,500 demonstrators were being held in custody.

Unable to cope with the seemingly unending flow of young people who were prepared to go to jail, Bull Connor turned to firehoses and dogs. His tactic had shifted from arrest to violent dispersal of the crowds.

The newspaper and television coverage of these events resulted in mounting expressions of sympathy for the demonstrators. On May 4, Attorney General Kennedy dispatched his chief civil rights assistant, Burke Marshall, to seek a solution to the conflict. King initially had reservations about the intentions of Marshall. In *Why We Can't Wait,* King comments:

> I was afraid that he (Marshall) had come to urge a 'cooling-off' period—to ask us to declare a one-sided truce as a condition to negotiations. To his credit, Marshall did not adopt such a position. Rather, he did an invaluable job of opening channels of communication between our leadership and the top people in the economic power structure.[18]

Interestingly, the negotiations were not with the city government officials, but rather with a group of approximately 125 businessmen. At first, they were reluctant to make any concessions. But as the jails were filled and the marchers remained firm in the presence of police violence, the Senior Citizens Committee realized that the movement could not be stopped.

On May 10, a truce containing four pledges was announced:

[18] *Ibid.,* p. 103.

to desegregate lunch counters, restrooms, fitting rooms, and drinking fountains, in planned stages within ninety days after signing;

to upgrade and hire Negroes on a nondiscriminatory basis throughout the industrial community of Birmingham, including the hiring of Negroes as clerks and salesmen within sixty days of signing and the immediate appointment of a committee of business, industrial, and professional leaders to implement an area-wide program for the accelerated upgrading and employment of Negroes in jobs previously denied them;

to cooperate with the movement's legal representatives in working out the release of all jailed persons, either on bond or personal recognizance; and

to officially establish communications between Negro and white through the Senior Citizens Committee or the Chamber of Commerce within two weeks after signing, so that further protests would be unnecessary.[19]

But the public announcement of peace did not bring peace. Segregationists were enraged that the Senior Citizens Committee had "sold-out to the niggers." On Saturday, May 11, the home of Reverend A. D. King, brother of Martin Luther King, was bombed. A few moments later, a bomb exploded outside the window of the room in the Gaston Motel where Dr. King had been staying. But King had left earlier for Atlanta. The bomb exploded just as the bars were closing in the Negro district. Enraged Negroes poured into the streets and began hurling rocks, wrecking cars, and setting fires.

These were not the same Negroes who had been marching nonviolently and filling the jails. But they were black brothers of Birmingham who had suffered the suppression and indignities of a white supremacist society, and the attempt on King's life triggered their rage.

Dr. King, with his nonviolent philosophy, had won a major victory. But in that moment of victory, violent white reaction gave birth to violent black reaction, a pattern that would repeat itself again and again.

The Birmingham confrontation is significant for two reasons. First, nonviolence had achieved its desired results. Operation C became a model for similar confrontations throughout the nation. The Justice Department counted 758 demonstrations in the ten

[19] *Ibid.*, pp. 105–106.

weeks that followed the Birmingham confrontation and 13,786 arrests in 75 Southern cities.[20]

But the Birmingham confrontation is also important because it marked the first time that a nonviolent protest involved Negro-initiated violence. King deplored the fact that violence had occurred. He deplored even more what he considered to be deliberate attempts of a few whites to incite the Negroes to violence. Nevertheless, violence had occurred and had assumed a role in the struggle for equality.

1964—A DREAM AND A LAW

On the heels of the Birmingham demonstration, the Kennedy administration considered legislation designed to allow greater participation of the Negro in American society. On June 19, 1963, President Kennedy sent a draft of his proposed civil rights law to Congress.

Realizing that the bill faced an uphill battle in Congress, civil rights leaders began planning a massive march on the nation's capital. The idea of the march originated with A. Philip Randolph, head of the Brotherhood of Sleeping Car Porters. The detailed planning fell to Bayard Rustin, former field secretary of CORE.

Rustin chose a broad theme—'For Jobs and Freedom'—to emphasize the necessity for improvement of the Negro condition in areas as diverse as unemployment, police brutality, education, housing, and other areas of discrimination. Every important Negro protest organization was represented in the march. In addition, many labor, church, and liberal groups were involved. The planners and participants were in agreement that nonviolence was essential for success.

On August 28, 1963, nearly 250,000 Americans converged on Washington for the day-long rally at the Lincoln Memorial. Estimates vary on the number who were white, but 30,000–40,000 was a commonly used figure. Some estimates placed the proportion of whites at one-third the total.[21]

The march was an impressive show of strength, demonstrating

[20] Theodore H. White, *The Making of the President 1964* (New York: Signet Books, 1966), p. 207.

[21] C. Eric Lincoln, *op. cit.*, p. 476.

cooperation, not only among Negro groups but between Negroes and whites. It also evidenced optimism about the Negro's future in America coupled with a plea for continued efforts to assure progress.

While the march had the unspoken blessing of the Administration, it failed to achieve the passage of the proposed civil rights legislation. The nonviolent show of support for the law was not sufficient to move it past numerous congressional stumbling blocks.

Not until after the assassination of John F. Kennedy, and then only with the determined executive leadership of Lyndon Johnson, did the proposal become law. Even so, the congressional debate was lengthy and acrimonious. Nine days of floor debate, totalling 73 hours and 41 minutes (477 pages of Congressional Record) in the House and 736 hours and 10 minutes of debate (2,890 pages) in the Senate were required.[22] But the bill which emerged was even stronger than that requested by President Kennedy. It provided:

Title I: strengthening the voting law of 1870;
Title II: reenacting and augmenting the public accommodations laws of the 1875 Civil Rights Act;
Title III: authorizing suit by the Attorney General of the U.S. to desegregate public facilities;
Title IV: authorizing authority as in Title III with respect to public schools;
Title V: authorizing the Attorney General to bring suit for an individual incapable of doing so himself and establishing a four-year Commission on Civil Rights;
Title VI: prohibiting discrimination in Federally assisted programs and providing for withdrawal of Federal funds where non-compliance persisted;
Title VII: prohibiting discrimination in employment by employers, employment agencies, and labor unions and establishing an Equal Employment Opportunity Commission;
Title VIII: requiring compilation of registration and voting statistics by the Secretary of Commerce;
Title IX: permitting the Attorney General to intervene in any civil rights lawsuit of general public import that is begun in a Federal court;
Title X: establishing a Community Relations Service to assist communities or persons involved in civil rights disputes; and

[22] Ianniello, *op. cit.*, p. 99.

Title XI: providing for jury trials and penalties for criminal con-
               tempts arising out of the enforcement of the act.[23]

On July 2, 1964, President Johnson signed the bill into law,
stating:

> The purpose of this law is simple. It does not restrict the freedom
> of any American so long as he respects the rights of others. It does
> not give special treatment to any citizen. It does say the only limit
> to a man's hope for his own happiness and for the future of his
> children shall be his own ability ... Its purpose is to promote a more
> abiding commitment to freedom, a more constant pursuit of justice
> and a deeper respect for human dignity ... Let us lay aside irrele-
> vant differences and make our nation whole.[24]

It seemed that nonviolence had again triumphed, albeit in the
face of grudging obstinancy. The march on Washington, coupled
with continuous but patient pressure on Congress, had achieved
the most all-encompassing piece of legislation on civil rights in
the nation's history. Significant progress had been made since
the Congress had decided in 1957 to merely study and develop
mechanisms for investigation. The Congress seemed ready to proceed with the business of enforcing equal opportunity. The Administration seemed ready to enforce the laws designed to end discrimination and segregation.

But many Negroes were growing impatient with the slow
progress toward racial justice in the nation, and they were not
convinced that the new legislation would change anything. Two
weeks after the signing of the Civil Rights Act, on July 16, 1964,
racial violence erupted in Harlem. Disturbances followed in Rochester, Jersey City, Paterson-Elizabeth, Chicago, and Philadelphia.

1965—A LAW AND A SHATTERED DREAM

In Selma, Alabama, only 355 of the city's 15,000 Negro residents were registered to vote in 1965. The Selma pattern was
typical of the state. Thus, in 1965, a nonviolent protest march,
from Selma to the state capitol in Montgomery, was organized to
dramatize voting discrimination.

Just outside Selma, the march was brought to a swift and violent

[23] Constance Baker Motley, "The Legal Status of the Negro in the
United States," in Davis, op. cit., pp. 487–488.
[24] Ianniello, op. cit., p. 99.

conclusion by law enforcement officers. The episode was captured by television cameras and transmitted into America's living rooms. The scene of brutal beatings and the use of tear gas on the marchers captured the conscience of the nation.

That same week, President Johnson addressed a joint session of Congress and the nation. He pleaded for new legislation to insure the right to vote for every citizen. Two days later, the President submitted a new bill for congressional consideration. The bill sought to plug still another gap in the Negro's quest for full participation in society. It had become too painfully obvious that the Civil Rights Acts of 1957, 1960, and 1964 failed to guarantee the Negro perhaps his most significant legal right. In his message to Congress, the President expressed his concern:

Our fathers believed that if this noble view of the rights of man was to flourish, it must be rooted in democracy. The most basic right of all was the right to choose your own leaders. The history of this country, in large measure, is the history of the expansion of that right to all of our people.

Many of the issues of civil rights are very complex and most difficult. But about this there can and should be no argument. Every American citizen must have an equal right to vote. There is no reason which can excuse the denial of that right. There is no duty which weighs more heavily on us than the duty we have to insure that right.[25]

The voting provisions of the original 1964 bill had contained measures to protect voting rights. By the time that law reached the President's desk, most of these measures had been eliminated by Congress. But the President was personally committed to the passage of these provisions:

I ask you to join me in working long hours, nights, and weekends if necessary, to pass this bill. And I don't make that request lightly. For from the window where I sit with the problems of our country I am aware that outside this chamber is the outraged conscience of a nation, the grave concern of many nations, and the harsh judgement of history on our acts ...

Their cause must be our cause, too. It is not just Negroes, but it is all of us, who must overcome the crippling legacy of bigotry and injustice ...

And so at the request of your beloved Speaker and Senator from Montana, the Majority Leader, the Senator from Illinois, the Minority Leader, Mr. McCulloch, and other leaders of both parties, I come here tonight—not as President Roosevelt came down one time in person

[25] *Ibid.*, pp. 116–117.

to veto a bonus bill, not as President Truman came down one time to urge the passage of a railroad bill—I come here to ask you to share this task with me and to share it with the people that we both work for. I want this to be the Congress, Republicans and Democrats alike, which did all these things for all these people.[26]

On March 21, the interrupted march to Montgomery began again. Three thousand men, women, and children—of both races —were on hand to continue the journey from the point where violence had ended it. In the interest of safety, the 3,000 were represented by 300 actual marchers. They marched for four days until they reached the outskirts of Montgomery. On the last four-mile leg of the march, the 300 were joined by over 50,000 Americans—from all parts of the nation—who had traveled to the capital of Alabama for a spectacular demonstration in support of the march's intent.

Again, the Congress did not act swiftly, but the complex legislative machinery had been prodded into action. On August 6, 1965, Lyndon Johnson signed the voting rights legislation into law.

President Johnson expressed his elation to the nation:

Today is a triumph for freedom as huge as any victory that's ever been won on any battlefield ...
This is a victory for the freedom of the American Negro, but it is also a victory for the freedom of the American nation. And every family across this great entire searching land will live stronger in liberty, *will live more splendid in expectation* (emphasis added) and will be prouder to be American because of the act that you have passed that I will sign today.[27]

Five days later (August 11, 1965), California Highway Patrolman Lee W. Minikus rode his motorcycle along 122nd Street, just south of the Los Angeles municipal boundary. A passing Negro motorist told the white officer that he had just seen a car being driven recklessly. Minikus gave chase and pulled the car over at 116th and Avalon, in the heart of a predominantly Negro neighborhood.

The driver of the car was Marquette Frye, a twenty-one-year-old Negro. His passenger was his older brother Ronald. Minikus ordered Marquette out of his auto to take the Highway Patrol's sobriety test. Frye failed and, at 7:05 P.M., Minikus placed him

[26] *Ibid.*, p. 119 and p. 124.
[27] Osofsky, *op. cit.*, p. 576 and p. 581.

under arrest. Minikus radioed for his motorcycle partner's assistance, for a squad car to take the younger Frye to jail, and for a tow truck to remove the now impounded auto. Frye's brother Ronald, told that he could not take the car while his brother went to jail, walked two blocks to their family residence. At 7:15 P.M., Ronald and his mother returned to the scene. Simultaneously, the second officer, the squad car, and the tow truck arrived.

It is not unusual for residents of the Avalon area to be outdoors on a warm California night. Initially, twenty-five to fifty curious spectators who happened to be nearby gathered to watch the proceedings of the sobriety test and subsequent arrest. By the time Ronald and Mrs. Frye arrived, the gathering of the curious had increased to about 250 or 300 persons.

Mrs. Frye scolded her son for drinking. He became belligerent, pushed her away, and moved toward the crowd shouting that the officers would have to kill him to take him to jail. The patrolmen pursued Marquette. He resisted. The crowd became hostile. The patrolmen radioed for help. When reinforcements arrived, all three Fryes were arrested. As the Fryes were being escorted to the squad car, someone in the crowd spat on one of the officers. Two highway patrolmen moved into the crowd, arrested a young Negro man and woman, charging they had created a disturbance and were inciting the crowd to violence. At 7:40 P.M., all the officers withdrew. As the squad cars pulled out, the last one to leave was pelted with stones by the now irate mob.

In forty minutes, an event had occurred which would scar the face of Los Angeles and usher in violence as a new form of protest in American cities. The Watts riot wore on for five days—144 hours. Calm was not restored until some 15,000 national guardsmen and 1,000 policemen occupied the area. The statistics were grim. Thirty-four persons had died and there were 1,032 reported injuries. A total of 3,952 adults and juveniles were arrested—almost three-quarters on charges of burglary and theft. Estimated property damage was 40 million dollars.[28] But these staggering statistics do not begin to measure the impact of the Watts riot. The Governor's Commission on the Los Angeles Riots titled their report, *Violence in the City—An End or a Beginning?* If there

[28] Statistics from: Report by the Governor's Commission on the Los Angeles Riots, *Violence in the City—An End or a Beginning?*, December 2, 1965, pp. 22–25.

was any doubt, the summers which followed answered the rhetorical question.

A great victory had been won in Washington. Nonviolence had achieved a further breakthrough—this time to guarantee the Negro his right to enter the mainstream of American life and tradition through the right to vote. Dr. King, seeing his dream realized bit by bit, later summed up the feelings of many Americans about the progress of the Civil Rights movement:

> The 1960 sit-ins desegregated lunch counters in more than 150 cities within a year. The 1961 Freedom Rides put an end to segregation in interstate travel. The 1956 bus boycott in Montgomery, Alabama, ended segregation on the buses not only of that city but in practically every city in the South. The 1963 Birmingham movement and the climactic March on Washington won passage of the most powerful civil rights law in a century. The 1965 Selma movement brought enactment of the Voting Rights Law ... Most significant is the fact that this progress occurred with minimum human sacrifice and loss of life.[29]

King might have had reason to be proud of the changes his nonviolent philosophy had wrought from a system of suppression that permeated much of the nation. Significant court action, administrative shows of force, and decisive legislation had taken place. He could even point to some real changes—at lunch counters and in bus depots, and in the critical area of the vote. But the signs of trouble in the rumblings of Negro violence in the summers of 1964 and 1965 and 1966 may have meant that King's summary of the successes of nonviolence would not be expanded. Perhaps the summary was in reality a conclusion, and a conclusion that bore the weight of a finality which would see nonviolence successful no more. If so, the dream of many more than Martin Luther King had collided with reality, the reality of a hundred places like Watts, and had shattered.

1966—ENTER BLACK POWER

In June, 1966, James Meredith was shot while leading a freedom march through Mississippi. Martin Luther King, Jr., Floyd

---

[29] Martin Luther King, *Where Do We Go From Here: Chaos or Community?* (New York: Harper & Row, Publishers, Inc., 1967), p. 58.

McKissick, Stokely Carmichael and others rushed to Mississippi to contest for the leadership of the march. When they reached Greenwood, Mississippi, the heart of SNCC territory, Carmichael proclaimed a slogan that would soon be the herald of a new phase in the Negro struggle: "What we need is black power." The fiery SNCC orator Willy Ricks, leaped to the platform and shouted over and over again: "What do you want?" With increasing fervor, the crowd answered: "Black Power."

Carmichael had not only chosen his locale carefully, he had carefully planned the moment. The presence of Dr. King and the flames that were bursting forth from the ghettoes gave him an immediate national forum.

Time was to make it somewhat clearer that 'Black Power' was not synonymous with 'Burn, Baby, Burn.' But it is also clear by now that threats of violence were not empty oratory. That non-violence no longer served as the sole theme of the Negro community became painfully obvious as the flames of racial disturbances licked voraciously at the nation's heels in forty major outbursts during the summer of 1966. The 100 or more outbursts in the summer of 1967 saw those same flames engulf the nation—with violence and with hate, to be sure—but also with confusion and fear.

By 1967, Dr. King was asking "Where Do We Go From Here?" The answer was by no means certain. More than one possibility presents itself as a potentially viable route. The white and black communities may now be searching their souls for the answer. And they may not.

Whatever the answer, it seemed by 1967 that the years of reason may have ended as the summers of violence began.

chapter three

A CHANGING MOOD?

THE FACT OF FRAGMENTATION

It is difficult for most white Americans to think of Negroes in terms other than monolithic stereotypes. Even the federal government, through the Census Bureau, groups Negroes into one statistical lump. These lumps become even more indefinite when Negroes are considered as part of the general category of non-whites.

Far more critical than the descriptive quandary into which these statistics place analysts are the resultant interpretive problems which arise, not only for the statistician, but also for the policy maker, social scientist, and even the general public. Who is the American Negro? What is his life really like? These are questions which themselves involve overgeneralizing. And the statistics available cannot provide more than superficial answers to already superficial questions. Faced with these difficulties, urbanologist Daniel P. Moynihan concludes in dismay:

... the lumping of all Negroes together in one statistical measurement very probably conceals the extent of the disorganization among the lower-class group. If conditions are improving for one and deteriorating for the other, the resulting statistical averages show no change.[1]

In the wake of Stokely Carmichael's 1966 proclamation of black

[1] United States Department of Labor, Office of Policy Planning and Research, *The Negro Family: The Case for National Action* (Washington, D. C.: Government Printing Office, 1965), p. 6.

power, the fragmentation of the 'community' of Negroes in America became more apparent than ever before. The progress of the Negro during the previous decade had not been uniformly impressive to all Negroes. In reality, disagreement over the type of progress desirable, the means necessary to achieve this progress, and the meaning of "progress" already achieved became more of an open source of conflict in the Negro community than even many Negro leaders expected.

The rise of the Black Muslims, the visibility of Negro radicals, and the re-evaluation of traditionally accepted Negro leaders can be understood in no other context than an explicit realization that the Negro community is itself in turmoil. It is not a homogeneous social, economic, political, or intellectual group of soul brothers.

The Negro responses to the late Dr. King's question "Where Do We Go From Here?" are quite varied, but in analyzing them, several hard realizations are inevitable. It seems increasingly evident that the Negro wants to answer the question of where and how he goes from here *for himself*. The white liberal who has assisted in the past has become for some a doubtful ally and for others, the enemy. Riots are not necessarily feared by Negroes. In fact many see violence as a necessity for progress—in much the same way that Marx viewed revolution, or that the framers of the Constitution viewed the democratic process of peaceful change. And, in these contexts, H. Rap Brown, Stokely Carmichael, Malcolm X, and Elijah Muhammad are not anomalies. Rather, they represent a viewpoint at one end of the spectrum of a continuing controversy—a viewpoint which is appealing to many Negro Americans. It may be that more and more Negroes are coming to reject the optimism Dr. King expressed about his people's future when, standing on the steps of the Lincoln Memorial, he said:

... in spite of the difficulties and frustrations of the moment I still have a dream. It is a dream deeply rooted in the American dream. I have a dream that one day this nation will rise up and live out the true meaning of its creed: "We hold these truths to be self-evident; that all men are created equal."[2]

[2] Martin Luther King, "I Have a Dream," address at the March on Washington, 1963; reprinted in Francis L. Broderick and August Meier (editors), *Negro Protest Thought in the Twentieth Century* (New York: The Bobbs-Merrill Company, Inc., 1965), p. 403.

Even then, in 1963, it was certain that there was disagreement with King's optimism on the part of other Negro leaders. Two weeks after the assassination of President Kennedy, Malcolm X, soon to be assassinated himself, addressed a rally at New York's Manhattan Center:

White America is doomed! Death and devastating destruction hang at this very moment in the skies over America ... The American government is trying to trick her twenty-two million ex-slaves with false promises that she never intends to keep. The crooked politicians in the government are working with the Negro civil rights leaders, but not to solve the race problem. The greedy politicians who run this government give lip service to the civil rights struggle, only to further their own selfish interests, and their main interest as politicians is to stay in power.[3]

The question, of course, is where the conflict stands today in the minds of that vast majority of Negroes who are not part of the elite group of Negro leaders. The answer is unknown. But there has been a related change in the rhetoric of the new and vocal Negro leaders. H. Rap Brown addressed a crowd in Cambridge, Maryland, during the summer of 1967. Police officials later charged that Brown's speech had incited the riot which ensued. Brown told the crowd:

America has laid out a plan to eliminate all black people who go against them. America is killing people down South by starving them to death in Alabama. Babies die. 500 people die a year for lack of food and nourishment. And yet we got enough money to go to the moon. Think about that. People in New York and Harlem die from rife [sic] and bites to death. Big old rats bite them to death and you tell the man about it and the honkey say: "Hell, man, we can't do nothing about them rats." Do you realize this is the same man who exterminated the buffalo. Hell, if he wanted to kill the rats he could do it.[4]

King's language had been eloquent, that of a scholar and practiced orator. Malcolm X's language had been sophisticated in its analysis of corruption in politics. Rap Brown's language was the

---

[3] Malcolm X, "God's Judgement of White America," a speech to a public rally at Manhattan Center in New York City, December 1, 1963; reprinted in *Evergreen*, December, 1967.

[4] H. Rap Brown, address at Cambridge, Maryland on July 24, 1967; reprinted in *Anti-Riot Bill—1967*, Hearings before the United States Senate Committee on the Judiciary, 90th Congress, First Session.

language of the streets—neither eloquent nor sophisticated. But his violent and angry words perhaps touched closer to the hearts of the mass of Negroes teeming in those streets than either King or Malcolm X.

The mood of the Negroes remains an open question. The juries of the streets are still out. Their verdict will answer Dr. King's question and determine, in large part, whether the future will be chaos or community as the struggle for equality continues.

Since 1954, significant *de jure* equality has been achieved. The goal is now to transform that legal equality into *de facto* reality— an equality in results. Negroes are no longer satisfied with merely having the law on their side. For legal equality does not insure that they will be allowed to enjoy its benefits. They want to achieve that measure of the society's abundance to which they believe they are entitled. Thus, the chance for a job is not enough. It must be a job which is commensurate with their skills, and a job which will provide an income large enough so that they and their families can enjoy the kind of life they perceive as desirable, as they see most of white America enjoying. If they lack requisite skills, they believe that the society which denied them even the hope for good employment in the past owes them the opportunity to acquire those skills. In like manner, the right to own a home is not enough. It must be a home of the kind and in the location of one's own choosing, not that which is left over after the white community has determined that certain types of homes and certain locations of residence are off-limits. So, too, merely teaching their children to read and to write is not enough. For those skills alone lead nowhere. A good life in the future for their children demands that they be educated in a manner that will prepare them for higher education or for a trade.

And the list goes on. In every area, it may seem to some that the Negro's demands for equality in results is an attempt to move too quickly into the mainstream of American life. Indeed, the indication is that this is exactly what they want to do: to move without delay so that another generation need not exist in poverty and misery. They demand only those things which white America has or is in the process of achieving.

But resistance to achievement of equality in results has been far greater than resistance to achievement of equality before the law.

Centuries of deprivation and prejudice have left their mark in social and institutional restrictions. *How* shall they overcome this new, greater, and far more complex resistance that derives not so much from legal as from social and institutional restrictions? A strategy is needed and decisions must be made.

Thus far, there is no consensus within the Negro community. Even individuals, as we shall see, have been torn by conflicting pressures to move towards more than one strategy simultaneously. Is it to continue to be King's nonviolence? Or will it be Carmichael's black power? Or Muhammad's black nationalism? While all three approaches disagree to some extent as to the final outcome, they have a common element in assertion of pride for the Negro—the man and the race. There are differences, of course, and they lie in the *means* which each advocates to achieve the goals. The purpose of this chapter is to probe the options and to develop a clearer understanding of the alternatives which the Negro community and its sub-groups have to choose from, as well as to analyze available data on the mood of the Negro community and its reactions to these alternatives.

MARTIN LUTHER KING AND NONVIOLENCE

Dr. King spent his college years studying philosophy and theology. This background molded his personal philosophy toward the nonviolent method of protest as the most successful strategy the Negro could employ to achieve social change in America. In *Stride Toward Freedom* (1958) he wrote:

In 1954 I ended my formal training with all of these relatively divergent intellectual forces converging into a positive social philosophy. One of the main tenets of this philosophy was the conviction that non-violent resistance was one of the most potent weapons available to oppressed people in their quest for social justice.[5]

In 1958, King saw six aspects of nonviolence as central to his thinking. They follow here in summary form:

1. *Nonviolence is not the coward's way out, because its aim is direct resistance.* It is a choice made from among alternatives:

[5] Martin Luther King, *Stride Toward Freedom: The Montgomery Story* (New York: Harper & Row Publishers, Inc.; Perennial Library Edition, 1964), pp. 82–83.

doing nothing, engaging in violence, or protesting nonviolently. It is a choice which is not a product of fear, but rather a choice requiring the strength of conviction. Nonviolence is not seen as "passive resistance" either; for, while the nonviolent resister is not physically aggressive, "his mind and emotions are always active, constantly seeking to persuade his opponent that he is wrong. The method is passive physically, but strongly active spiritually."

2. *Nonviolence doesn't seek to defeat or humiliate the opponent, but to win his respect and understanding.* "The end is redemption and reconciliation. The aftermath of nonviolence is the creation of the beloved community, while the aftermath of violence is a tragic bitterness."

3. *The resistance is levelled not against persons engaging in evil but rather against the evil itself.* The nonviolent protester seeks to defeat injustice, not the persons "victimized by evil."

4. *The nonviolent resister must be willing to accept violence to himself without retaliation,* to "accept blows from the opponent without striking back."

5. *The nonviolent protester avoids not only physical but also spiritual violence.* He "not only refuses to shoot his opponent but he also refuses to hate him. At the center of nonviolence stands the principle of love." This principle of love is based upon an understanding of humanity such that if any man is hurt, all men are burdened by the pain and suffering of his injury.

6. Finally, *nonviolent protest is based upon a conviction that history is on the side of justice.* Thus, the protester is confident of his eventual success because of the righteousness of his stand. "... he knows in his struggle for justice he has cosmic companionship ... Whether we call it an unconscious process, an impersonal Brahman, or a Personal Being of matchless power and infinite love, there is a creative force in this universe that works to bring the disconnected aspects of reality into a harmonious whole."[6]

What King has outlined is an attitude with deep religious significance. Before that nonviolent attitude could be effective it had, to be transformed into a plan for action. King explicated the steps involved in that activation:

[6] *Ibid.*, pp. 83–88.

In any nonviolent campaign there are four basic steps: collection of the facts to determine whether injustices exist; negotiation; self-purification; and direct action.[7]

The first two steps are self-explanatory; however, the third step, self-purification, has a special meaning. Before direct action is taken, each nonviolent protester must undergo a period of self-examination to condition himself in the acceptance of the principles of nonviolence. Once this is done, the protester may then engage in direct action designed to call attention to the injustice and to create enough discomfort in a community so that a positive response is elicited.

The final desired response is once again negotiation of and action upon the grievance. In fact, at each level of activity, negotiation is seen as a desirable alternative to protest. In his "Letter from a Birmingham Jail," King explains:

You may well ask: "Why direct action? Why sit-ins, marches, and so forth? Isn't negotiation a better path?" You are quite right in calling for negotiation. Indeed, this is the very purpose of direct action. Nonviolent direct action seeks to create such a crisis and foster such a tension that a community which has constantly refused to negotiate is forced to confront the issue. It seeks so to dramatize the issue that it can no longer be ignored.[8]

King's patience, determination, and optimism resulted from his two-fold faith in nonviolence. *Theoretically*, nonviolence can create enough of a crisis to produce negotiations for a satisfactory resolution of the injustice. *Historically*, King sees parallels of successful nonviolence on the part of other oppressed peoples:

The religious tradition of the Negro had shown him that nonviolent resistance of the early Christians had constituted a moral offensive of such overriding power that it shook the Roman Empire. American history had taught him that nonviolence in the form of boycotts and protests had confounded the British monarchy and laid the basis for freeing the colonies from unjust domination. Within his own century, the nonviolent ethic of Mahatma Gandhi and his followers had muzzled the guns of the British Empire in India and freed more than three hundred and fifty million people from colonialism.[9]

[7] Martin Luther King, Jr., *Why We Can't Wait*, p. 78. Copyright 1964 by Martin Luther King, Jr. Reprinted by permission of Harper and Row, Publishers.
[8] *Ibid.*, p. 79.
[9] *Ibid.*, p. 37.

STOKELY CARMICHAEL AND BLACK POWER

The concept of black power is not a doctrine of religious significance, as is nonviolence. Instead, it is a Machiavellian analysis of political power and group behavior within the framework of a neo-Marxian dialectic for social change.

In their provocative book, *Black Power*, Stokely Carmichael and Charles Hamilton see black power as the most effective way in which the Negro can advance his position in America today. The route for the Negro to achieve progress is strong quasi-political organization: organization aimed at achieving black power.

But first the Negroes in America must unify into a cohesive bloc, putting an end to their currently fragmented status. In a pluralistic society such as ours, any minority group which seeks to be politically successful in advancing itself must first establish itself as a unified, hard core group, capable of forming or joining a winning bloc or coalition. This bloc or coalition is essential for political progress.

The concept of Black Power rests on a fundamental promise: *Before a group can enter the open society, it must first close ranks.* By this we mean that group solidarity is necessary before a group can operate effectively from a bargaining position of strength in a pluralistic society. Traditionally, each new ethnic group in this society has found the route to social and political viability through organization of its own institutions with which to represent its needs within the larger society.[10]

To form such a cohesive group, however, black power advocates needed a common unifying theme, something that all Negroes could identify with themselves. Not surprisingly, the theme chosen has been pride in being Black: "Black is beautiful." Attached to this theme is an identification with the Negro's African heritage. Carmichael and Hamilton continue:

Studies in voting behavior specifically and political behavior generally, have made it clear that politically the American pot has not melted. Italians vote for Rubino over O'Brien; Irish for Murphy over Goldberg, etc. This phenomenon may seem distasteful to some, but it has been and remains today a central fact of the American political system. There are other examples of ways in which groups in the

[10] From *Black Power* by Stokely Carmichael and Charles V. Hamilton. © Copyright 1967 by Stokely Carmichael and Charles V. Hamilton. Reprinted by permission of Random House, Inc.

society have remembered their roots and used this effectively in the political arena ... The extent to which black Americans can and do "trace their roots" to Africa, to that extent will they be able to be more effective on the political scene.[11]

Once this unity is achieved, black America must struggle to convince the American nation, now permeated with white supremacy, that black people are capable of doing things for themselves. Thus, the self-identification of Negroes as a black community allows that community to press for self-determination—in business, in government, and in every other field.

There is no necessity for this self-assertion of blacks as blacks to lead to "racism in reverse." Black power, according to its advocates, would be successful at that point in time when white America accepted black America as equal. Not equal in the sense that blacks have conformed to what many consider abhorrent white patterns of living, however; for the Negro sees himself, under the banner of black power, as an intelligent, capable individual, able to maintain or establish his own patterns of living and his own value structures and norms. However, should the movement toward effective black power result in racism in reverse, the advocates of the movement are not overly concerned:

In the end, we cannot and shall not offer any guarantee that Black Power, if achieved, would be non-racist. No one can predict human behavior. Social change always has unanticipated consequences. If black racism is what the larger society fears, we cannot help them. We can only state what we hope will be the result, given the fact that the present situation is unacceptable and that we have no real alternative but to work for Black Power. The final truth is that the white society is not entitled to reassurances, even if it were possible to offer them.[12]

Once the community has unified behind the banner of black power, if it does, the question turns upon the goals that should be sought by the Negro in his quest for progress. Integration is rejected, because it is seen as tantamount to assimilation into white society, an acceptance of middle-class white attitudes, conditions, life-styles, and so on. This further means that the Negro must abandon his own culture and heritage which, as it has thus far

[11] *Ibid.*, pp. 44–45.
[12] *Ibid.*, p. 49.

developed, is somewhat outside the mainstream of white, middle-class mores. For the advocate or supporter of black power, to abandon his own mores for those of middle-class white America is to live a contradiction. Perhaps the ultimate goal of black power is the reduction of the importance of color itself. However, if 'color-blindness' is to be the goal, it assumes the same kind of acceptance of black people as has been accorded other minority groups as they became accepted into society as equals. Namely, it assumes that Negroes will be allowed to maintain their 'Blackness' as much as the Irish have maintained their 'Irishness' and the Italians have maintained their 'Italianness.' The final result would then be a Negro community, no longer with colonial status, but rather an accepted and acceptable part of American society, equal in every way to other ethnic and minority groups now enjoying the fruits of the nation's plenitude. Say Carmichael and Hamilton:

"Integration" also means that black people must give up their identity, deny their heritage. We recall the conclusion of Killian and Grigg: "At the present time, integration as a solution to the race problem demands that the Negro forswear his identity as a Negro." The fact is that integration, as traditionally articulated, would abolish the black community. The fact is that what must be abolished is not the black community, but the dependent colonial status that has been inflicted upon it.[13]

Within this context, Negroes who have achieved 'progress' by assuming middle-class white standards, as well as Negro leaders who teach that integration in terms of assimilation into white society is desirable, are seen as traitors to the cause of the Negro. They attempt to escape their 'Negroness' by identification with and acceptance of the values of white society. In effect, they have abandoned their roles as Negroes. When Carmichael and Hamilton discuss such Negroes, they place them in nearly the same class of enemy as the general white community.

It is crystal clear that most of these people have accommodated themselves to the racist system. They have capitulated to colonial subjugation in exchange for the security of a few dollars and dubious status. They are effectively lost to the struggle for an improved black position which would fundamentally challenge the racist system.[14]

[13] *Ibid.*, p. 55.
[14] *Ibid.*, p. 14.

The relationship between black power and violence is clear. Negroes cannot allow white supremacy to oppress them any longer. To do so means to relegate the masses of Negroes to a continued colonial status of exploitation, pacified only by token gains achieved through the political system. Violence is seen as a potentially necessary alternative because peaceful change through the political system is slow and by no means certain. This is especially true since black power advocates see the political system itself as a tool of white supremacists—a tool which white America has effectively used to deny black America all but token gains.

For the black power advocate, time has run out; assertion of his pride and his *de facto* equality demand changes that will produce significant results—now:

> Those of us who advocate Black Power are quite clear in our own minds that the "non-violent" approach to civil rights is an approach black people cannot afford and a luxury white people do not deserve. It is crystal clear to us—and it must become so within the white society—*that there can be no social order without social justice.* White people must be made to understand that they must stop messing with black people, or the blacks *will* fight back![15]

ELIJAH MUHAMMAD AND BLACK NATIONALISM

The movement of The Nation of Islam began early in the 1930's with the preachments of Prophet W. D. Fard, purportedly an immigrant from Arabia, to Negroes in Detroit. When Fard mysteriously disappeared in 1933, Elijah Muhammad became the movement's leader and spokesman. E. U. Essien-Udom, noted scholar of the movement, points out that in its early days The Nation of Islam had a relatively small following:

> For more than two decades the Nation of Islam was a small, highly secretive group known to few Negroes. Its activities and influence expanded immensely during the years 1954–1961, however, and Muhammad now bids openly for the allegiance of the Negro masses of the country.[16]

By nature, the movement is essentially religious, structuring itself around the beliefs of Islam. However, there are important distinctions between the movement and the traditional conception

---

[15] *Ibid.*, p. 53.
[16] E. U. Essien-Udom, *Black Nationalism: A Search for Identity in America* (New York: Dell Publishing Company, Inc., 1964), p. 19.

of Mohammedanism. For example, Prophet Fard, not Mohammed, is acknowledged by Elijah Muhammad and his followers as the Mahdi, or messiah, of the movement. The religious overtones are *Muslim*, not *Moslem*.

The primary doctrine of the Muslims is the concept of black nationalism. Essien-Udom explains:

> The concept of nationalism ... may be thought of as the belief of a group that it possesses, or ought to possess, a country; that it shares, or ought to share, a common heritage of language, culture, and religion; and that its heritage, way of life, and ethnic identity are distinct from other groups. Nationalists believe that they ought to rule themselves and shape their own destinies, and that they should therefore be in control of their social, economic, and political institutions. Such beliefs among American Negroes, particularly among the followers of Muhammad, are here called black nationalism.[17]

There are several ramifications of this conception of black nationalism. First, every American Negro is potentially a member of The Nation of Islam. To assume his place in the 'nation,' each Negro must develop a consciousness of nation, an awareness of his role as part of a group that is distinct. A concomitant of this awareness of nation is similar to an element of black power: to develop a consciousness of nation, the Negro must develop a pride in his blackness, overcoming the tradition of slavery and oppression with its perpetuation of a feeling of inferiority on the Negro's part.

Second, the white man has created a myth of white supremacy in order to exploit the black man. The Muslims have a prophetic view of the downfall of the white man and his myth: Allah, a black man, has determined that the white man will meet his downfall in the year 1970. At that time, the Negro and all other colored races throughout the world will rise up and take their rightful places of supremacy.

Third, the Nation of Islam lacks a territorial base. It is believed that the antecedents of black nationalism are to be found in the Arabian civilization. There is no planned program for the establishment of a political territorial home. Rather, vague religious prophecies are relied upon as offering assurance that a territorial home will eventually be found.

Fourth, to aid the Negro in establishing the requisite feeling

---

[17] *Ibid.*, p. 20.

of pride, a strict moral code, reminiscent of early Puritanism, is advocated. Followers are urged to be pure, hard-working, clean, industrious, honest, etc. Prayer, reverence, and a trust in Allah are essential, for the prophecies of black supremacy are inevitable.

Fifth, as a consequence of their religious view of inevitable black nationalism as supreme, the Muslims advocate strict segregation of the races. Middle-class Negroes—the Black Bourgeoisie of E. Franklin Frazier—who aspire to assimilate themselves into the white American traditions are seen as having 'sold out,' in ignoring and attempting to escape their blackness—which is in reality their true and ultimate salvation. Only a separate society, apart from white men, will allow black nationalism to flourish as it inevitably must. Before his break with Elijah Muhammad, Malcolm X said with conviction:

> White America refuses to study, reflect, and learn a lesson from history; ancient Egypt didn't have to be destroyed. It was her corrupt government, the crooked politicians, who caused her destruction. Pharoah hired Hebrew magicians to try and fool their own people into thinking they would soon be integrated into the mainstream of that country's life. Pharoah didn't want the Hebrews to listen to Moses' message of separation. Even in that day separation was God's solution to the "slaves problems." By opposing Moses, the magicians were actually choosing sides against the God of their own people.[18]

The implications of the statement should be obvious. The traditional civil rights leader who attempts to achieve the goal of integration is no better than the magician. Those who follow these traditional leaders are, at best, foolishly misguided. Those who, on the other hand, follow the direction of the Muslims will, like the Jews, eventually triumph over their oppressors. And all whites are oppressors without exception. Even those white liberals who seem to advocate the Negro's advancement are insidious enemies. Malcolm X:

> In this deceitful American game of power politics, the Negro (i.e., the race problem, the integration, and civil rights issues) are nothing but tools, used by one group of whites called *Liberals* against another group of whites called *Conservatives*, either to get into power, or to remain in power ... The white liberal differs from the white conservative in only one way: the liberal is more deceitful than the conservative. The liberal is more hypocritical than the conservative. Both want

[18] Malcolm X., *loc. cit.*

power, but the white liberal is the one who has perfected the art of posing as the Negro's friend and benefactor; and by winning the friendship, allegiance, and support of the Negro, the white liberal is able to use the Negro as a pawn or tool in this political football game that is constantly raging between the white liberals and white conservatives.[19]

White liberals and white conservatives are equally insidious because both advocate white supremacy, although one is more adept at using the Negro's disadvantaged condition to maintain that supremacy.

The religious and nationalistic fervor inspired by the racist implications of Muslims are in ways reminiscent of Nazi Germany and Imperial Japan. The Muslims, convinced of their favor with Allah, see the world in terms of *black and white in conflict*. They are confident that in the end, black will be on the side of virtue, right, and victory. White, segregated according to the Muslim plan, will lose its supremacy based on the evil of Negro inferiority that white temporarily created.

THE NEGRO MOODS

Negroes have mixed feelings about these philosophies. Response to King's nonviolence, Carmichael's black power, and Muhammad's black nationalism, as well as other options of strategy has not been clearcut. While there may be a community consensus on the need for advancement, the specific goals of advancement and the means to be employed in their achievement are still subjects of controversy.

The ambivalence of the individual Negro to the varied strategies may be seen in James Baldwin's *The Fire Next Time*. Baldwin describes his meeting with black nationalist leader Elijah Muhammad, his invitation from Muhammad to join the Muslim movement, and, in this passage, his feelings upon rejecting the invitation:

It was time to leave, and we stood in the large living room, saying good night, with everything curiously and heavily unresolved. I could not help feeling that I had failed a test, in their eyes and in my own, or that I had failed to heed a warning. Elijah and I shook hands, and

[19] *Ibid.*

he asked me where I was going. Wherever it was, I would be driven there—"because, when we invite someone here," he said, "we take the responsibility of protecting him from the white devils until he gets wherever it is he's going." I was, in fact, going to have a drink with several white devils on the other side of town. I confess that for a fraction of a second I hesitated to give the address—the kind of address that in Chicago, as in all American cities, identified itself as a white address by virtue of its location. But I did give it, and Elijah and I walked out onto the steps, and one of the young men vanished to get the car. It was very strange to stand with Elijah for those few moments, facing those vivid, violent, so problematical streets. I felt very close to him, and really wished to be able to love and honor him as a witness, an ally, and a father. I felt something of his pain and his fury, and yes, even his beauty. Yet precisely because of the reality and the nature of those streets—because of what he conceived as his responsibility and what I took to be mine—we would always be strangers, and possibly, one day, enemies. The car arrived—a gleaming, metallic, grossly American blue—and Elijah and I shook hands and said good night once more. He walked into the mansion and shut the door.[20]

The vivid encounter described by Baldwin typifies part of the quandary of the Negro in choosing an appropriate option. Confronted with the offer of a militant, black segregationist strategy, Baldwin could not accept. He understands Muhammad, and even admires him. He cannot dispute much of what Muhammad says:

And I looked at the young faces around the table and looked back at Elijah, who was saying that no people in history had ever been respected who had not owned their own land. And the table said, "Yes, that's right." I could not deny the truth of this statement.[21]

And he realizes that at best the man he admires and understands will always be aloof from him—at worst, the man will be his enemy. But Baldwin must forego Muhammad's friendship, for Baldwin cannot conceive of the Negro as having a place separate from American society. He himself has labored too long to try to aid his race in establishing that place within America. Yet, he listened to Muhammad, understood, and was impressed by him—especially in his appeal to the wellspring of pride in his race.

Muhammad, too, is ambivalent. His large mansion, his spacious

---

[20] Reprinted from *The Fire Next Time* by James Baldwin (pp. 92–93). Copyright © 1962, 1963 by James Baldwin and used by permission of the publisher, The Dial Press, Inc.

[21] *Ibid.*, p. 87.

living room, his "gleaming, metallic, grossly American blue" auto, his handshake at the parting—all raise questions: how separated can Muhammad be from the society he so hates? Could the Negro, even under ideal circumstances, create a society separate and distinct from the underlying values of white America which have been foisted upon the Negro in over 400 years of quasi-assimilation? The evidence from the brief portrait of Muhammad's own life indicates not. Perhaps for Muhammad, as well as for Baldwin, some things remain "curiously and heavily unresolved."

But Baldwin is a leader, and Muhammad is a leader. Each of them, and many others, has followers of one sort or another, as do other leaders. But how many? And what do their followers really believe? What of those others who are unsure? The moods of the masses of Negroes have been studied and often.

But perhaps not often enough, or with the right techniques of measurement and analysis. On first glance, which is about all the attention most Americans pay to them, the surveys show little need for concern. Even after several years of summer riots, the Negro majority seems to reject everything but the slow, rational, non-violent route to equality. Surprisingly enough, some of the studies show Negroes and whites in essential agreement on the course of Negro progress. A Louis Harris poll taken for *Newsweek* in the summer of 1967 showed that both blacks and whites were "in essential agreement" on the following conclusions:

The riots have hurt the Negro cause.
Negroes themselves suffer worst in the rioting.
Most Negroes do not support the ghetto rioting.
Looting and fire-bombing are criminal acts.
Large-scale Federal programs to set up summer camps for young-sters and work programs for the unemployed, to eradicate rats and tear down urban ghettos, would be effective measures against future racial disorders.[22]

Fortune published the following conclusions of a survey of 300 Negroes in thirteen cities (an average of twenty-three per city) in the winter of 1967:

Three out of four Negroes feel that their condition is better than it has been in recent years.

[22] "After the Riots: A Survey," *Newsweek*, August 21, 1967, p. 18.

Eight out of ten think their chances of getting a good job are better, and on the controversial matter of housing, seven out of ten think conditions have improved.

Three out of four feel more hopeful that Negroes' problems will be solved; a mere four per cent are less hopeful.[23]

The mood of these conclusions is highly optimistic. At question is the critical issue of whether or not the mood of the surveys represents the mood of the Negro. Methodologically and analytically, the polls are open to significant criticisms.

Turning to the question of methodology, how were the Negro attitudes determined?

The first critical problem in conducting surveys of the kind mentioned is drawing a representative sample. There is serious doubt that a reliable sample of the Negro population is ever located by those conducting the interviews for the polls. In his controversial report on "The Negro Family," Moynihan notes the impossible task of finding many Negro men in the ghetto, particularly those who have withdrawn from even the subculture of the slums. Looking specifically at the data of the 1960 U.S. Census, he writes:

Donald J. Bogue and his associates, who have studied the Federal count of the Negro man, place the error as high as 19.8 percent at age 28; a typical error of around 15 percent is estimated from age 19 through 43. Preliminary research in the Bureau has resulted in similar conclusions, although not necessarily in the same estimates of the extent of the error. The Negro male *can* be found at age 17 and 18. On the basis of birth records and mortality records, the conclusion must be that he is there at age 19 as well.[24]

Consider, for a moment, that young adult males are often identified as participants in riots. If these individuals, as a consequence of their withdrawal from the Negro community as a whole, are excluded in the Census Bureau's sampling, how likely is it that their opinions will be represented in far less comprehensive studies such as the *Newsweek* and *Fortune* examples? With a 15–20 per cent error in the Census, it is likely that even a random selection of houses in a ghetto will fail to turn up a significant proportion of

[23] Roger Beardwood, "The New Negro Mood," *Fortune*, January, 1968, pp. 146–147.

[24] U. S. Department of Labor, *op. cit.*, p. 43.

the more alienated social drop-outs. Therefore, their attitudes—which may be critical in terms of the total picture of Negro moods—are never registered.

A second problem in measuring the attitudes of Negroes is the validity of the responses those Negroes who are reached in the sample give to the interviewer. Does an interviewer approaching a Negro ghetto dweller with a set form of questions immediately influence the type of response the interviewee will give, so that it fails to reflect the individual's true feelings? As we shall see in a moment, the phrasing of the particular questions in the survey may produce answers which do not really reflect the respondent's feelings correctly.

In like manner, will a Negro answer a white interviewer with the truth or, will he tell a white man what he believes the white man wants to hear? To avoid this problem, many surveying companies have employed Negroes to interview other Negroes in the ghetto. But the problem is not necessarily eliminated. Is it possible that the ghetto dwellers see the Negro interviewers (who are generally better educated than the ghetto dwellers) as sell-outs or pawns of the white man; that they perceive the use of members of their own race to elicit information from them as a further example of white exploitation of blacks?

These problems give us serious reason to question the reliability of these surveys. Moreover, the public is generally presented only with the compiled answers and conclusions. And, too often, writers stress the conclusions that it would seem the public wants to hear.

Which leads us to a second important question: how valid is the interpretation of the results compiled in these surveys? Assume for the moment that the 1963 and 1966 *Newsweek* surveys[25] of Negro sentiments accurately reflect the moods of Negroes. How valid are the analysis and conclusions which are drawn from the data collected?

In the 1963 and 1966 studies, Brink and Harris analyzed Negro approval of various leaders. Their report (see Table 1) concludes that Martin Luther King had the overwhelming support of Negroes in both years.

[25] William Brink and Louis Harris, *Black and White* (New York: Simon and Schuster, 1966). Copyright © 1963 by Newsweek, Inc. Selections following are reprinted by permission of Simon and Schuster, Inc.

TABLE 1

How Negroes Rank Their Leaders

Rank and file Percentage Approving			Leadership Group Percentage Approving	
1966	1963		1966	1963
88	88	Martin Luther King, Jr.	87	95
71	79	James Meredith	35	81
66	80	Jackie Robinson	58	82
64	68	Roy Wilkins	62	92
56	60	Dick Gregory	65	80
54	X	Charles Evers	68	X
53	62	Ralph Bunche	49	87
48	64	Thurgood Marshall	81	94
47	X	James Farmer	70	X
44	51	Adam Clayton Powell	49	52
35	X	A. Philip Randolph	83	X
33	X	Whitney Young, Jr.	70	X
22	X	Bayard Rustin	53	X
19	X	Floyd McKissick	35	X
19	X	Stokely Carmichael	33	X
12	15	Elijah Muhammad	15	17[26]

Note: X not on 1963 list

Brink and Harris conclude:

Clearly, Martin Luther King remains the preeminent leader; where it is possible to make comparison, every other leader has slipped since 1963. And Stokely Carmichael and Floyd McKissick come in near the very bottom of the list.[27]

For them, the evidence clearly indicates far greater support for the tactics of the nonviolent King, as opposed to the militant strategy of Carmichael. Brink and Harris explain the discrepancy between the response of the rank-and-file and the leadership group by pointing to the greater likelihood that the leaders would recognize some of the names and to the greater impatience of the leaders than the rank-and-file:

True, King himself has slipped somewhat with the leadership sample, and these men also rate Carmichael and McKissick higher than

[26] *Ibid.*, p. 54.
[27] *Ibid.*

does the rank-and-file. In part, this is because they are more likely to have heard the names of the newcomers—the recognition factor, in other words. But it also is a reflection of the fact that the leadership group is a great deal more impatient and willing to turn to the new militants like Carmichael and McKissick. In another question of the survey, 43 percent of rank-and-file Negroes say the pace of the revolution is too slow, but an overwhelming 82 percent of the leadership group feels the pace is not fast enough.[28]

It is possible that the leadership group more freely expresses its true attitudes than do the rank-and-file; that, in fact, the rank-and-file are also more militant-oriented than the survey shows. But, that methodological question aside, Brink and Harris fail to recognize the possibility that the lessening of support for King and the increase of support for the militants among the leadership group might be an indication of something more than a simple recognition factor or simply impatience—that it might, in fact, be an indication of a full-scale re-evaluation of the nonviolent approach and its potentials for success as compared to the more militant approaches and their chances for success.

As for the rank-and-file, a more detailed analysis of the Brink and Harris survey results (results contained in the Appendices, but never analyzed or stressed publicly) show some disturbing possibilities. One question asked Negroes to evaluate the work done by a series of individuals. The results shown in Table 2 appeared.

What is startling is the significantly large proportion of Negroes who were not sure of their thoughts about the work of men like Carmichael and Muhammad. Once Stokely Carmichael had made his black power proclamations (too late to be included as a leader in 1963's survey), there was apparently great uncertainty over his approach. The answers in this survey indicate that Negroes had not yet, in 1966, decided whether or not to commend or condemn Carmichael. The same is, to a great degree, true of the work of Muhammad.

Three factors could account for this seemingly overwhelming uncertainty within the Negro community. First, there could be a serious lack of knowledge about these leaders. Second, there could be an unwillingness on the part of the respondent to admit to an

[28] *Ibid.*, p. 55.

TABLE 2

NEGRO EVALUATION OF WORK DONE BY THREE NEGRO LEADERS

	Martin Luther King[29]		Stokely Carmichael[30]		Elijah Muhammad[31]	
	Percentage of Total		*Percentage of Total*		*Percentage of Total*	
	1966	**1963**	**1966**	**1963**	**1966**	**1963**
excellent	75	78	7	X	4	5
pretty good	13	10	12	X	8	10
only fair	2	3	8	X	7	6
poor	1	1	5	X	36	29
not sure	9	8	68	X	45	50

interviewer that the respondent has established an opinion one way or the other. And, third, there could be a genuine ambivalence on the part of the individual, because he might in some respects support a man like Carmichael, but for various reasons be unwilling to admit, even to himself, his true feelings.

The likelihood of a lack of information about a man like Carmichael seems relatively small. His advocacy of black power in June of 1966 has received national attention in the news media frequently enough to make him a household word. Before that time, he had been an outspoken leader of SNCC. It would certainly seem that his reputation would filter down into the ghetto by the time of the 1966 survey, conducted through the summer months of that year. But, perhaps it did not. If it did, the large percentage of Negroes unsure about his position indicates that at least his position was then being considered.

In the case of Elijah Muhammad, the recognition problem seems of less relevance. He had been a leader of black nationalism since the mid-1930's and, as previously noted, had begun making open appeals throughout Negro America for support as early as 1954. Once again, the large percentage of persons in the Negro community unsure as to Muhammad's desirability would seem to indicate a serious problem for them in determining their response.

[29] *Ibid.*, p. 246.
[30] *Ibid.*, p. 244.
[31] *Ibid.*, p. 248.

However, in 1963, a considerable percentage did feel that he was doing a poor job. And the percentage increased by 1966. Evidently, some of those who had previously seen him as doing an excellent job, a pretty good job, or who were uncertain had re-evaluated their positions, and their verdict had not been in favor of black segregation.

Brink and Harris conclude that the tenets of black power as well as black nationalism are out of tune with the Negro mood:

> Any assessment of the chauvinistic new philosophy of black power must conclude that—as the *Newsweek* survey showed—it is out of step with the views of the majority of Negroes.[32]

It is questionable that such an interpretation follows from the data (again, found only in the Appendices) that were gathered. In 1966, Negroes were asked whether they favored or opposed the concept of black power. The results were:

Favor 25%   Oppose 37%   Not Sure 38%[33]

First, with a distribution such as this, it seems impossible to conclude that any views are those of the majority of Negroes. But, more important, a full one-quarter of the respondents expressed support for black power. With nearly 40 per cent undecided, Brink and Harris are stretching their data to fit their conclusion. It is possible that the undecided individuals in 1966 might be leaning toward black power, though not firmly behind it. In that case, black power would most certainly be in the mainstream of Negro thoughts and attitudes.

Compared to the results of similar questions on black nationalism and on the Black Muslims in particular, the doctrine of black power actually fared quite well, as the 1966 survey results show:

	Black Nationalism[34]	Black Muslims[35]
Approve	5%	4%
Disapprove	63%	66%
Not Sure	32%	30%

The above results correspond quite closely to the evaluations expressed about those in the Negro leadership group who represent

[32] *Ibid.*, p. 65.
[33] *Ibid.*, p. 264.
[34] *Ibid.*, p. 260.
[35] *Ibid.*, p. 262.

the varying philosophies or strategies. On Stokely Carmichael and black power, a large percentage are unsure, but a significant percentage indicate approval. On Elijah Muhammad and black nationalism or Black Muslims, a large percentage are unsure, but a significant percentage indicate disapproval.

Just as Baldwin could take pride in some of the tenets of black nationalism, as advocated by the Muslims, so too it seems that a considerable proportion of the Negro community shares such pride. But, just as Baldwin was forced to reject the Muslims and their black segregation as impractical, so too a large portion of the Negro community seems to reject the nationalist approach. Not so with black power. The 1966 survey does not give conclusive proof that black power is out of line with the Negro's thinking and feelings. Rather, the results indicate a strong pocket of support in the Negro community for black power, as well as an undecided group which could swing toward or away from it. This is not to say that black nationalism or the Muslims are irrelevant to the Negro: for the fact of his inability to come to a firm value judgment upon either indicates that a large percentage of the Negro community may still be considering it as a potential option.

The work of Gary Marx on Negro militancy would tend to validate the conclusion that, while not in ascendance, black nationalism and the Muslims are far from a dead issue:

> Our data indicate that, when an individual or an organization was disapproved of, it was almost certain to be Malcolm X and the Black Muslims. Still, consistent with the above statement, about one-half of those questioned did not offer disapproval of either.[36]

Other surveys have shown similar results: namely, that black power and black nationalism are getting significant degrees of consideration from undecided Negroes. All too often, however, these other surveys similarly bury the somewhat disconcerting findings amidst optimistic conclusions. In the 1967 *Fortune* survey the general conclusions indicate that the Negro's status in America is improving. Hidden among those optimistic conclusions are indications that the Negro is anything but satisfied with the progress that nonviolence has achieved for him.   For example:

[36] Gary T. Marx, *Protest and Prejudice* (New York: Harper & Row, Publishers, Inc., 1967), p. 109.

Almost half are more angry than they were a few years ago, and only about one in ten is less angry.

A majority endorsed the Reverend Martin Luther King's aggressive nonviolent tactics; but over a third endorse more violent methods. Northern Negroes put somewhat more emphasis on violence than southern urban Negroes do.[37]

The Negro is here seen as more angry and more prone to violence—indications that black power, if not black nationalism, is getting more consideration than was the case only a year earlier.

After the riot in Detroit in 1967, the *Free Press* conducted a survey among the city's Negroes. The *Free Press* was forced to conclude:

Most Detroit Negroes believe that there could be another riot ... Eighty-four percent of those queried in the Urban League survey said that a riot like the one that began a month ago could happen again. Eleven percent were not sure.[38]

While this result does not indicate that a majority support the violence that may come, it does resubstantiate that more Negro violence is not by any means beyond consideration.

Contrary to the conclusions of the writers, the results of surveys like those in *Fortune* and the *Free Press* do not give the white community reason to be assured that all is well. The specific question asked in the *Fortune* survey was "Are violence and rioting necessary to achieve Negro objectives?" Not only do over a third endorse violent methods, they see them as essential. This, in light of the Detroit finding that more violence is expected, casts serious doubt upon the conclusion of many surveys that "Negroes still support the nonviolent position of Martin Luther King."

Nonetheless, King was consistently ranked high on questions eliciting responses of trust and approval. How to reconcile this fact with an apparent movement away from nonviolence toward the more militant strategies of civil rights is a crucial question. The answer may lie in King's symbolic appeal to the Negro. When Harris asks, "How would you rate the job the individual has done?" or *Fortune* asks, "Does the individual fight for what the Negro wants?" there is no assurance that a positive response

[37] Roger Beardwood, *loc cit.*
[38] "Most City Negroes Think Riot Could Happen Again," Detroit *Free Press*, August 22, 1967.

answers the really critical questions: "Is this individual's method a feasible one for you to use in achieving your goals? Do you see validity in the position of other Negro leaders? Are you irrevocably committed to nonviolence?" As Lomax observes:

... Martin Luther King's role is that of a symbolic leader. Martin is to the Negro revolt what Paul was to the early church ...[39]

To disapprove of King would be tantamount to disapproving of a Christ-symbol, a martyred saint. Thus, it is entirely possible that Negroes may identify with the symbolic King and approve of him, and at the same time be influenced by and attracted to the preachments of Carmichael and Muhammad.

A final problem for the surveys and for the America they inform is hinted at in the critical question asked above: namely, "Are you irrevocably committed to nonviolence?" Surveys can generally only measure attitudes at a specific point in time. Only by follow-up surveys, competently designed and analyzed, can changes in attitudes be observed. The critical question, at both the leadership level and the rank-and-file level, is the direction in which the Negro community's attitudes are moving.

The truth is that in a scientific sense we don't really know what the Negro mood is or how it may be shifting. We lack data, such as that provided by political polls, which take a continuous reading of the ghetto temperature. Moreover, for reasons we have indicated, it is questionable whether such polling procedures can produce reliable or very precise data.

In the absence of systematic survey data, we have to rely on other sources to interpret the ghetto mood. The reports of militant leaders may not be the most reliable source. They tend to surround themselves with other angry black men and it is not clear that they have their finger on the pulse of the ghetto. They tend to see what they want to see just as the white reporter tends to look for disapproval of militancy and signs of hope in the ghetto.

Perhaps the most significant indicator is to be found in looking at the moderate Negro leadership. Entertainers, such as Harry Belafonte, Sammy Davis Jr., and Bill Cosby, have been shunned by the more militant Negroes as Uncle Toms who have sold out

[39] Louis E. Lomax, *The Negro Revolt* (New York: Harper & Row, Publishers, Inc., 1962), p. 92.

to the white man's system. Nevertheless, many Negro entertainers, athletes, and other public figures, have been quietly involved in the civil rights movement for many years. What is significant is that many of them, who have in the past avoided public pronouncements on the racial issues, are becoming much more vocal. And their voices are cries of anger and warning to the white community that time is running out.

Negro leaders in almost every field seem to be increasingly reluctant to denounce the most militant spokesmen. Rather, they seem to be saying that the H. Rap Browns and the Stokely Carmichaels are a product of a racist society, and unless white America changes, we can expect to see an increasingly militant mood.

Writer James Baldwin, who respected, but was unable to join Elijah Muhammad, also has deep respect for Stokely Carmichael. In an interview in *Esquire* he tries to interpret Carmichael to a predominantly white readership:

Stokely is a leader for a great many people. Stokely is even more than that, Stokely is a *symbol* for a great many people. A great many emasculated black boys turn to Stokely because he's fighting against their emasculation. I understand that, and they're right. I may have my own disagreements with Stokely from time to time but I'm on his side. What Stokely is saying essentially is true and that is why people are so uptight about Stokely. Because they can't deny what he is saying.
... What he is suggesting that frightens the American white people is that the black people in this country are tied to all the oppressed and subjugated people everywhere in the world. Furthermore, he is saying very clearly, and it's true, that this country which began as a revolutionary nation has now spent god knows how many billions of dollars and how many thousands of lives fighting revolution everywhere else. And what he's saying is that black people in this country should not any longer turn to President Lyndon Johnson, who is after all at the very best (and this is an understatement; I'm speaking for myself now) a very untrustworthy big daddy. But to other black people, all the other people who are suffering under the same system that we are suffering from, that system is led by the last of the Western nations. It is perfectly conceivable, or would be if there were not so many black people here, that the Americans might decide to "liberate" South Africa. Isn't it? That is to say, to keep the horrors of communism away, all the freedom fighters in South Africa would turn South Africa into another Vietnam. No one is fooled about what you are doing in Vietnam. At least no black cat is fooled by it. You

are not fighting for freedom. You don't care about those people. You don't care about my people and I know you don't care about theirs. You're fighting for what the Western world calls material self-interest. And that means my back. My stolen tin, my stolen diamonds, my stolen sugar. That's what it means; it means I should work for you forever.

And I won't.

But the idea is that people who are divided by so many miles of globe, and by so many other things, should begin to consider themselves as a community, should begin to consider that they have something in common—this is what Stokely says. What they have in common is to get the man off their backs. It's very dangerous and frightening idea for Americans, because it happens to be true.[40]

Jim Brown, former Cleveland Browns football great turned movie actor and founder of the Negro Industrial and Economic Union, talked with a *Playboy* interviewer about Carmichael and Rap Brown:

I feel there is a need for them. Unfortunately, the average white seems to need a good scare from the Carmichaels and Rap Browns before he'll listen to less dramatic requests. Speaking for myself, I think it's too easy to just go out and threaten Whitey. What is that doing to help black people? At the same time, I've been turned down by so many Administration officials, seeking money and support for our self-help program—and not just turned down but suspected of being 'subversive'—that I've been tempted to take the easy way, too, and start hollering against Whitey myself. As long as Administrations refuse to sponsor programs that give black people constructive alternatives to violence, I can't really blame these guys for their extremism. I think they symbolize a lot of those their age who are sick of passive resistance, who are really fighting for freedom—young Negroes with great pride in themselves and their race ... Like them or not, they are what the white man is going to have to deal with more and more. They're brash and fearless and they're going to fight in any and every way they feel necessary to be respected and to win their freedom in this country.[41]

Dr. Kenneth Clark, distinguished psychologist and educator, talked with Mary Harrington Hall, then Managing Editor of *Psychology Today*, shortly after the assassination of Dr. Martin Luther King.

Clark's approach to the racial crisis is more scholarly and

[40] *Esquire*, July, 1968, p. 52. Reprinted by permission of *Esquire* magazine. Copyright © 1968 by Esquire, Inc.

[41] *Playboy*, February, 1968, p. 63.

analytical than most Negro spokesmen, but his mood reflects the same sense of seriousness and urgency:

We may not survive. American society is suffering from a very serious, very severe disease. A disease which, for want of a better word, I would call moral schizophrenia.[42]

Mary Hall asked Dr. Clark:

Why, when we all knew there would be blood in the streets last summer, were no massive programs undertaken to try and prevent the ghetto riots?[43]

Dr. Clark's reply:

Because this nation is playing Russian roulette. We know there's a bullet there, but we take a chance. It's easier for the White to keep taking the chance than to deal with the kind of massive social therapy that is necessary. Remember, ghetto life and what pass for schools in the ghetto produce bitter young people with absolutely nothing to lose in the conflagration of your cities. They don't believe in anything. They don't give a damn about anything ...
... They will continue to burn. It's a poetic form of social mathematics. There seems to be an irresistible relationship between injustice and retribution, even when it involves self-destruction. It's the Negroes who are being killed ... What the American people have to learn is that they really can't destroy Negroes without destroying themselves.[44]

Even Dr. Martin Luther King, Jr., a man who reaffirmed his personal commitment to nonviolence the night before he was slain, seemed to understand that the movement was passing from his hands and that he could not control the increasing anger and frustration. In a *Look* article, which was on the newsstands when he was killed, Dr. King wrote:

I'm convinced that if something isn't done to deal with the very harsh and real economic problems of the ghetto, the talk of guerrilla warfare is going to become much more real. The nation has not yet recognized the seriousness of it. Congress hasn't been willing to do anything about it ... As committed as I am to nonviolence, I have to face this fact: if we do not get a positive response in Washington, many more Negroes will begin to think and act in violent terms.[45]

[42] *Psychology Today*, June, 1968, p. 19. © 1968 by CRM Inc.
[43] *Ibid.*, p. 20.
[44] *Ibid.*
[45] Martin Luther King, Jr., "Showdown for Nonviolence," *Look*, April 16, 1968, p. 25. © 1968 by the Estate of Martin Luther King, Jr. Reprinted by permission of Joan Daves.

In a very real sense, nonviolence vs. violence is becoming an irrelevant issue. It is overridden by a growing and irreversible impatience to be free. There seems to be an emerging unity among black people. Some may not approve of violence or themselves ever engage in violent behavior, but they can understand why some of their brothers feel driven to extreme measures. They may feel that there are better avenues to achieve their common goals than violence. But at the same time they can't be certain. Nonviolence has been a long and painful road, and the gains have been slow in coming. There are risks in violence—the most serious being genocide—but perhaps it will achieve victories which have eluded nonviolence.

A changing mood? The pollsters seem to think not. Only a small minority are engaged in looting and burning. The large majority, they tell us, are opposed to violence. But perhaps their lumping of a significant proportion of "undecided" responses into the same category with those favoring nonviolence is a kind of statistical sophistry. It is hard to look at the intensified pace of violence these past summers, it is hard to listen to moderate Negro leaders, and it is hard to walk the streets of the ghetto and not sense a changing mood.

Perhaps the large majority of Negro Americans still believe in nonviolence. But they are also becoming increasingly aware of the fact that white America has not done well by them. The large majority may never burn or take up arms to fight an impossible revolution. But this does not mean that they are not growing angry with the system. Those who are committed to violence as a strategy for change will find recruits in the ghettoes—especially among the young who have heard the promise of a new day, but tasted only frustration, bitterness, suppression, and broken promises.

chapter four

FROM PLANTATION TO GHETTO:
A Continuing Tragedy

THE SOULS OF BLACK AND WHITE

In 1903, W. E. B. DuBois posed the following critical consideration:

> Between me and the other world there is ever an unasked question: unasked by some through feelings of delicacy; by others through the difficulty of rightly framing it. All, nevertheless, flutter around it. They approach me in a half-hesitant sort of way, eye me curiously or compassionately, and then, instead of saying directly, How does it feel to be a problem? they say, I knew an excellent colored man in my town; or, I fought at Mechanicsville; or, Do not these Southern outrages make your blood boil? At these I smile, or am interested, or reduce the boiling to a simmer, as the occasion may require. To the real question, How does it feel to be a problem—I answer seldom a word.[1]

DuBois had brilliantly captured an essential element of race relations in America: The Negro in America has been considered by white America to be and, in many ways, is a problem. His very presence has been disquieting to the conscience of white America. As a slave, the Negro in a land of the free was a contradiction in the most basic principles of an entire society. As a man, some-

---

[1] W. E. Burghardt DuBois, *The Souls of Black Folk* (Greenwich, Connecticut: Fawcett Publications, Inc., 1961), p. 15. Reprinted by permission of Fawcett Publications, Inc.

67

how considered different in ways unrelated to his skin color, he placed white America in a quandary as he sought participation in a white-controlled system of government and a white-dominated society. And, as a man, he is—or at least has seemed to be —unsure of himself. Unsure in questioning his own status as an equal to the white man, and unsure in seeking an answer to the question of why he must struggle to improve his status by moving up from the place in society to which white America has assigned him.

Although the Negro and the white man perceive the problem differently, there is only one racial problem in America, only one set of objective events. Although these events have been reacted to with different attitudes and have had differing impacts on black and white America, the interaction of these events, the actions, attitudes, and impacts they have produced, form one pattern. As President Johnson told a Joint Session of Congress in March of 1965:

> There is no Negro problem. There is no Southern problem. There is no Northern problem. There is only an American problem.[2]

This chapter is an attempt to trace the continuing development of "the problem" from the plantation to the ghetto where it has reached crisis proportions.

SLAVERY

The first Negroes to touch the shores of what now constitutes America were not slaves. Rather, they were participants in the great explorations of the several European nations which had embarked upon the road to discovery. Some of the Negroes participating in these ventures were of relatively high social status. One such man was Estevanillo, a leader in the ill-fated expedition of the Spaniard de Narvaez. Only four members of the 1527 expedition survived,. three of them eventually returning to Spain. Estavanillo remained as a medicine man among the indigenous

[2] Lyndon B. Johnson, "Remarks to a Joint Session of the Congress, March 15, 1965," as reprinted in Lynne Ianniello (editor), *Milestones Along the March* (New York: Frederick A. Praeger, Publishers, 1965), p. 16.

population. His adventures later gained him credit for the discovery of the Zuni Indians and the territory of New Mexico.

The first appearance of Negroes in the English colonies of the New World occurred in 1619. This time, they were not members of expeditionary crews, but slaves. Twenty Negroes were purchased by the settlers in Virginia from a Dutch man-of-war. During the seventeenth and early part of the eighteenth centuries, slavery, as an institution, was not a distinct and systematic procedure. It was considered to be analagous to the common practice of indentured servitude, by which many poor Europeans agreed to work for others for a specified period of time in return for payment of transport from Europe to the colonies.

By the end of the eighteenth century the system of indentured servitude had virtually come to an end, and slavery as an institution achieved prominence in its stead. Slavery had already established a legal identity in the Virginia and Maryland colonies, distinguishing it from indenture, by the end of the seventeenth century. By the end of the eighteenth century, large numbers of slaves were being imported into the colonies.

The following data, compiled from Census records beginning in 1790, indicate the size of the slave population up to the time of the Civil War.

Census Year	Slave Population
1790	697,624
1800	893,602
1810	1,191,362
1820	1,538,022
1830	2,009,043
1840	2,487,355
1850	3,204,313
1860	3,953,760[3]

Federal law formally prohibited the importing of slaves after 1808. Until this time, the international slave trade flourished on American shores. Historian Henry Carey's analysis of ship records and port reports indicates the magnitude of the trade. This com-

[3] Reprinted with permission of the Macmillan Company from *The Negro in the United States* by E. Franklin Frazier, p. 39. Copyright 1949 by The Macmillan Company.

parison of Census records and the records of slave importation deserves comment.

Time	Number of Slaves Imported	Average per Year
Prior to 1715	30,000	....
1715–1750	90,000	2,500
1751–1760	35,000	3,500
1761–1770	74,500	7,400
1771–1790	34,000	1,700
1791–1808	70,000	3,900
TOTAL	333,500	....[4]

Carey accounts for 333,500 imported slaves by 1808. In 1810 the Census enumerated 1,191,362 slaves, or a discrepancy of almost 860,000. Two factors must certainly contribute to an accounting for these additional 860,000 slaves. First, ship records and port records were almost certainly inadequate. But even so, the natural reproduction of slaves during this period had to be incredible, and these figures lend credence to historical accounts of widespread forced slave breeding—much as livestock are reproduced.

After 1808, the *major* increase in the slave population was in all probability natural growth. Estimates of the number of additional slaves imported before 1860 range from 300,000 to one million, but by 1860 the Census enumerated almost four million slaves in the United States. Considering the fact that infant mortality and poor health conditions took a heavy toll, the birth rate of slaves during this period had to be among the highest of any group of people in human history.

The powerful impetus for enslavement of the black man could not be explained simply by his physical differences. Strong economic motivations, particularly in the South, added significantly to the strength of the slave system. As Frazier explains:

The fact that the Negroes were an alien race bearing distinctive physical marks was, doubtless, the basis for differential treatment from the beginning and later facilitated their enslavement. But it was not

[4] Henry C. Carey, *The Slave Trade* (1853), cited in Gunnar Myrdal, *An American Dilemma* (New York: Harper and Row, Publishers, 1944), p. 118.

due solely to difference in race that Negro slavery grew and finally supplanted white servitude. There were powerful economic factors, such as the demand for a cheap and permanent labor supply, that decided the fate of the Negro. Court decisions and statutes only gave legal sanction to customary practices or what was becoming an established fact. Later, because of the invention of the cotton gin, and the rise of the textile industry in England, the slave system became the foundation of the economic life of the South. When for economic as well as moral reasons, slavery was attacked by the North, the Bible and political philosophy were invoked to give an absolute sanction to the slave system.[5]

Census data also detail the number of *free* Negroes in the United States until the time of the Civil War.

Year	Free Negroes	Percentage of Negroes in United States Who Were Free
1790	59,557	7.9
1800	108,435	10.8
1810	186,446	13.5
1820	233,634	13.2
1830	319,599	13.7
1840	386,293	13.4
1850	434,495	11.9
1860	488,070	11.0[6]

In 1790 only 7.9 per cent of American Negroes were free men. This figure rose to 13.7 per cent by 1830, but then began to decline. By 1860, only 11 per cent were free. Thus, during this seventy-year period approximately nine of ten Negroes were slaves: for most, to be black meant to be a slave.

The 1863 Emancipation Proclamation ended slavery as a formal legal institution. As a social reality it did not end until much later. The system which had made slavery a keystone of the Southern economy would not easily break down. Even the years of Reconstruction did not significantly affect the status of most Negroes, for they did not have the skills, or financial resources to do anything but remain on the plantations—and for those few Negroes who did have the skills or financial resources, there

[5] Frazier, *op. cit.*, p. 22.
[6] *Ibid.*, p. 62.

were few opportunities. They were freed *de jure* but *de facto* they remained slaves.

The Compromise of 1877 and the subsequent withdrawal of Union troops from the South opened the door for the insidious system of Jim Crow segregation and its continuing and systematic degradation of the Negro. Just as slavery had been both a legal and a social phenomenon, so too was the segregation and second-class citizenship of the Negro under Jim Crowism a legal and social phenomenon. Not until the opportunities of a highly industrial economy emerged before World War I, and the opportunities for masses of Negroes to migrate to the North and West, did the Jim Crow system in the South begin to weaken. But, even as it weakened in the South, the pattern of degrading segregation took a stronger foothold in the North and West, a foothold that grew into a system such that today, some claim, the servitude and oppression of the Negro is no less real than it was in the ante-bellum South.

While attempts have been made to minimize the tragedy of slavery, the horror inherent within the American slave system cannot be ignored or stressed too strongly. The white man did not exterminate the Negro, for he was a valuable economic resource; but he did strip him of nearly every reason for human existence. The sub-human conditions of transport, the inhuman chattel status of the slave, the destruction of his culture, family, and pride are all a part of the atrocities that slavery systematically developed. The brutality, both mental and physical, of the slave system insured that any black man who experienced it would serve to prove that the myth of black inferiority had been harshly transformed into an imposed reality.

The parallels between this tragic chapter in American history and the extermination of the Jews by the Nazis cannot be escaped. White America used the same rationalizations the Nazis used to justify the Negro's inferiority: biological inferiority, threat of inbreeding, uselessness in 'civilized' society, etc. The parallels are obvious. The major difference is that the white man in America condemned his victims to a living death. The impact of this tragedy cannot be dismissed or forgotten if one is to understand the continuing struggle of the American Negro for selfhood and identity. The slave system may have been formally ended nearly a century ago, yet the system continues to leave its ugly scars in baseless feelings of white superiority and the endless struggle of blacks to find their own self identity. Indeed, its subtleties continue to warp the entire fabric of American racial relations. That white America fails to understand this only exacerbates the problem.

MIGRATION AND URBANIZATION

Patterns of migration cannot fail to have an impact upon a nation's development. In the case of the massive Negro migrations from the South to locations in the North, the impact was made not only upon the future of race relations within the nation, but also upon the Negro himself.

The Census of 1860 shows 94.9 per cent of the Negroes in the United States living in the South (which included Missouri in the count of that year). Only one-tenth of 1 per cent lived in non-Southern states west of the Mississippi. The remaining 5 per cent were located in Northern states east of the Mississippi.

Precise patterns of migration in the country are very difficult to trace. The freedom of mobility across state lines, without specific checks and tabulations of the characteristics of the travelers, allows an analysis only of the results of a continuous flow of persons. Decennial census data give only approximate results, showing the final location of persons and groups of specified types after ten years of movement.

But the general patterns of movement are abundantly clear. The Negro moved:

out of the South to the North (and later to the West);
from predominantly rural to highly urbanized areas;
and experienced increasing concentration in high density segregated slum ghettos.

OUT OF THE SOUTH

A complete picture of these trends can be traced in the Census Bureau statistics. Around 1915, the migration of the Negro from the South began to increase heavily. Between 1910 and 1920 the net migration of Negroes out of the South totaled 454,300.[7] For the next four decades, large numbers continued to flee from the South. Only in the decade of the Great Depression did the pace of the exodus slacken, as the figures below indicate:

Decade	Number of Negroes Leaving South
1920–30	749,000
1930–40	347,500
1940–50	1,244,700
1950–60	1,457,000

In 1860, 94.9 per cent of the nation's Negro populace lived in the South. A century later, in 1960, only 54 per cent of the nation's Negroes remained in the South; 19 per cent lived in the Northeast states, 19 per cent lived in the North Central states, and 8 per cent lived in the West.[8]

While historians and demographers have not fully agreed upon the primary factors causing the upsurge in migration after 1915, it seems fairly clear that several factors are of considerable relevance. All of them probably played a part in diffusing the nation's Negro population throughout its states.

First, poor whites began to infiltrate the labor market, pushing some Negroes out of employment in even the most menial of jobs in the South.[9] Second, the cotton growing industry, which still employed many Negro hand laborers, moved slightly westward in its focus. The ravaging boll weevil took its toll on the Southern cotton economy, eliminating the need for as large a labor force as was previously required. A similar impact was registered by a severe drought striking the cotton industry, and other agricultural concerns, during 1916 and 1917. The draft for World War I caused the moving of a large number of Negro men from their home communities. And, finally, the demand for labor in the North, generated by the drafting of white workers, the closing off

[7] For a more detailed discussion of Negro migration patterns see: Karl E. Taeuber and Alma F. Taeuber, "The Negro Population in the United States," in John P. Davis (editor), *The American Negro Reference Book* (Englewood Cliffs, New Jersey: Prentice-Hall, Inc., 1966), pp. 108–115.

[8] U. S. Department of Labor, Bureau of Labor Statistics, *The Negro in the United States* (Washington, D. C.: Government Printing Office, 1966), p. 4.

[9] These factors are detailed in: Myrdal, *op. cit.*, pp. 191–196.

of foreign sources by immigration restrictions, along with the war's requirement for generally increased industrial production, all meant that Northern industry had to actively seek out Negro labor in the South and—obviously—sought it out quite successfully.

As the momentum of the great migration grew, each of these factors probably began to play a greater role in the individual Negro's decision to stay or leave. If friends or neighbors concerned about continued employment in the South ventured northward, it became easier for a man to use the same rationale and to turn to the same solution. Agents of Northern industries promising Negroes specific jobs and providing railroad fare northward presented strong incentives. The communications of friends and neighbors, who had jobs in the North, and who told of the new and somewhat promising lives they led, were commonly circulated throughout the Negro community in the South. The Negro press, printing advertisements, news stories, and editorial commentaries favorable to the northward move, added to the promise of a new and different and better life outside the South.

Obviously, no one individual was affected by all these factors. However, together the factors created a situation which tended to push the Negroes from the South and to pull them toward the North. The discrepancy between the North and South in terms of opportunity and hope for the black American continued to widen as the mass northward migration gained momentum. The attractiveness of leaving the South for a new life in the North prompted more and more Negroes to overcome the inertia and fear which had tied them to the South.

But despite what might seem to be overwhelming pressures for leaving, particularly the history of poor treatment, there were still strong counteracting pressures operating on the Southern Negro to stay. Social ties were particularly strong. Leaving behind family and friends to travel to far off and certainly strange places was not an appealing prospect for many. Others held employment in the South and were skeptical (in many cases, quite justifiably) of opportunities promised by the move North. As Karl and Alma Taeuber note, these factors operated in a manner which made the decision to migrate a phenomenon most pronounced among young Negro males:

Migration is a highly selective process. Young adults are usually much more eager to give up the old for the new than are those with families, homes, and secure attachments to customary ways of living.[10]

Thus it was that between 1920 and 1930, forty-five out of every 100 Negro males between the ages of fifteen and thirty-four left the state of Georgia. Between 1940 and 1950, Mississippi lost nearly half of its young Negro males through migration. The impact of this selective movement may be inferred by looking to Northern census data which shows that in 1920, 1930, and 1940, 30 to 50 per cent of the young Negro males had moved to their Northern residences within the previous ten years.

In summary, the migration of the Negro out of the South continued steadily from 1915 to 1930, slackened somewhat as the promise of jobs in the North during the Depression dwindled, resumed strongly in response to the war-created demand for labor during World War II, and is continuing now as a consequence of the post-war boom and continued industrial and economic prosperity.

INTO THE CITIES

In 1910, prior to the snowball of migration out of the South, 73 per cent of the nation's Negroes, compared with 52 per cent of the whites, lived in rural areas (locales with less than 2,500 inhabitants). By 1960, urbanization was more predominant among Negroes than whites, with 73 per cent of the Negroes and only 70 per cent of the whites residing in urban areas. As sociologist Philip Hauser notes:

... within a period of fifty years, less than a lifetime, the Negro has been transformed from a predominantly rural to a predominantly urban resident. In fact, in 1960, Negroes were more highly urbanized than whites ...[11]

As a consequence, in 1960, the six United States cities with the largest concentrations of Negroes held almost 20 per cent of all the Negroes in the nation.[12]

---

[10] Taeuber and Taeuber, *op. cit.*, p. 112.

[11] Philip M. Hauser, "Demographic Factors in the Integration of the Negro," in Talcott Parsons and Kenneth B. Clark (editors), *The American Negro* (Boston: Houghton Mifflin Company, 1966), p. 75.

[12] U. S. Department of Labor, *The Negro in the United States*, p. 3.

Broadening the focus of analysis to metropolitan areas (Standard Metropolitan Statistical Areas or SMSA's), instead of examining simply rural-urban differences, makes the fact of the Negro's metropolitanization even more startling. In 1910, only 29 per cent of the nation's Negroes lived in SMSA's. By 1960, this figure had increased to 65 per cent. Comparing the increases in metropolitan concentrations for Negroes and whites shows that between 1920 and 1940, Negroes living in SMSA's increased by 65 per cent as compared with 36 per cent for whites—and, between 1940 and 1960, Negroes increased by an astounding 109 per cent as compared with 50 per cent for whites.[13]

If we restrict our examination of Negro population growth in urban areas to the *central cities* only, the redistribution and concentration of blacks becomes even more apparent. Hauser describes the process:

Between 1910 and 1920, the Negro population in central cities of metropolitan areas increased by 40 per cent; between 1920 and 1940, by 83 per cent; and between 1940 and 1960, by 123 per cent. Hence, by 1960, 51 per cent of all Negroes in the United States lived in the central cities of SMSA's. Of all Negroes resident in metropolitan areas, 80 per cent lived in central cities. There was a much higher concentration of Negroes in metropolitan areas and in their central cities in the North and West than in the South. In 1960, of all Negroes in the North 93 per cent were in SMSA's and 79 per cent in the central cities; and in the West 93 per cent in SMSA's and 67 per cent in central cities. In the South, however, 46 per cent of all Negro residents lived in SMSA's and 34 per cent in central cities. Finally, it must be observed that Negroes are disproportionately concentrated in the large SMSA's and especially in their central cities. The twenty-four SMSA's with 1 million or more persons in 1960 contained 38 per cent of the total Negro population, and their central cities, 31 per cent. Comparable figures for whites are 34 and 15 per cent.[14]

In Increasing Numbers

It must be remembered that the Negro in America today is a member of a minority group, representing approximately 11 per cent of the nation's total population. But it must not be forgotten that the 11 per cent figure makes the Negro the nation's largest minority group. Moreover, this figure camouflages the fact that in some areas the Negro is in the majority.

[13] Hauser, *op. cit.*, p. 76.
[14] *Ibid.*

Differentials in birth rates, both black and white, and in immigration regulations have played a large part in determining the exact proportion of America's population which is black. The percentage has fluctuated between a low of 9.7 per cent (1930) and a high of 14.1 per cent (1860) over the last century. While the 14.1 per cent in 1860 represented approximately 4.5 million Negroes, the 1960 rate of 9.9 per cent places the absolute number of Negroes today at some twenty million.[15] Sheer numbers would make the Negro a critical variable for the nation's future, even were the nation color-blind.

IN GROWING CONCENTRATIONS

It is not unusual for immigrants to cluster together. The security of being among the people and the ways of the familiar past is often sought and found in such clusters. In almost every major American city, colonies of German, Irish, Italian, Chinese, etc., are by no means uncommon.

There are definite parallels between the initial residential location of European immigrants and the location patterns of Negroes moving North. The 1920 Census data, for instance, indicate that in New York City, Chicago, Philadelphia, Detroit, Cleveland, and Pittsburg, the most recent immigrants (Poles, Lithuanians, Italians, and Greeks) were concentrated in isolated settlements as were the Negro residents of these cities.

But the Italian, as well as the Irish, the Pole, the German, etc., eventually became assimilated to some extent within the general population of the city. The immigrants began to improve their status culturally and economically. Second generation immigrants found themselves equipped with better educations and as a result, were able to secure and hold better jobs and maintain a higher standard of living than were their parents. With these status improvements, a large proportion of the ethnic populations began to disperse into the larger metropolitan entity—leaving only small colonies of nationality neighborhoods.

But this same process has not happened to the Negro immigrant. He has remained economically and culturally deprived. Even when

---

[15] U. S. Department of Commerce, Bureau of the Census, *Statistical Abstract of the United States, 1966* (Washington, D. C.: Government Printing Office, 1966), p. 22.

he has made significant gains on the education and economic
ladders, his easily distinguishable color has made it easy for a
prejudiced society to discriminate against and exclude him from
the larger metropolitan area.

An educated Irishman, who conformed to the standards of
middle class society, lost most of his "objectionable" ethnic traits.
The Jew, who wanted to move outside of the Jewish ghetto, could
change his name. The Italian could get rid of his accent. But the
Negro cannot escape his color—his high visibility makes him a
target of discrimination even after he has economically achieved
middle class status and socially internalized the values of middle
class society. His only physical mobility has been, and for the
most part remains, within a black ghetto—a city within a city.

The development of Harlem is an interesting case study in the
development of one of these concentrations into a black ghetto.[16]

In the early 1900's Harlem had been overbuilt with large new
apartment houses, apartments planned for white occupancies. However, the lack of rapid transportation to the Harlem area caused
landlords great difficulties in filling the dwellings on Harlem's east
side. An enterprising Negro real estate dealer proposed to several
of the white landlords the possibility of filling the empty residences
with steady Negro tenants. The landlords accepted Philip Payton's
suggestion, and, gradually, Negroes began moving in.

The extent of this 'encroachment' began to frighten white residents of Harlem. In response, they proposed the formation of the
Hudson Realty Company. The purpose of the company was simple:
buy all the properties occupied by Negroes and evict the tenants.
But the Negroes in New York City, pooling their resources at
times, countered the white strategy with precisely the same tactics.
As the contest continued, whites began to fear an invasion of blacks,
became panic stricken, and fled, leaving in their wake sometimes
entire blocks of deserted dwellings. When the landlords' mortgages
began to default on the empty units, banks and mortgage companies were compelled to foreclose and operate the apartments
themselves.

For a considerable period of time, these operators preferred to

---

[16] For a more detailed discussion of the development of the Harlem
ghetto see: Gilbert Osofsky, *Harlem: The Making of a Ghetto* (New York:
Harper & Row, Publishers, 1965); and Myrdal, *op. cit.*, pp. 1125–1126.

hold the properties vacant rather than to rent or sell to Negroes. Values continued to drop, reaching their all-time low just as war was breaking out in Europe. Negroes in the New York area, and particularly in those areas of Harlem where they had been allowed to maintain residency, continued to build a black community, establishing churches, social clubs, and civic centers. As the financial institutions holding title to the remaining Harlem apartments saw that either a perpetual loss of returns on committed capital or the prospects of renting or selling to Negroes were their only options, they made the obvious choice.

Gradually, Harlem changed from a middle-class residential area, built for whites, to a Negro ghetto, occupied by blacks, and—finally—to a cesspool of misery, trapping the oppressed.

In other Northern cities, the same pattern occurred. Different historical events accounted for particular clustering, but in each city the concentration of Negroes—whether by choice or by white designation—appeared. At first, with only small numbers of Negroes moving North, black colonies often formed near the homes of the rich that many Negroes served. Later, as more Negroes moved North, creating a mounting demand for housing, established Negro areas developed as whites fled. Almost always, the Negroes, like other newcomers to American cities, inherited the most deteriorated and undesirable areas. In 1960, census data indicate that most large cities confined at least half, and often more than half, of their Negro populations to census tracts in which 90 per cent or more of the residents were black and in which population densities per square mile were unusually high. Besides being confined to living with only other blacks, the Negro was confined in a disproportionately small space for his numbers. And even that small space was generally adjacent to other spaces similarly crowded with Negro residents, so that the inordinately large number of blacks in the inordinately small locations formed one or more pockets of overly crowded humanity within the city itself.[17]

Several studies have thoroughly documented the patterns of segregation within our urban areas. Duncan and Lieberson[18] analyzed ethnic and racial segregation in Chicago for 1930 with an

---

[17] U. S. Department of Labor, *op cit.*

[18] Otis Dudley Duncan and Stanley Lieberson, "Ethnic Segregation and Assimilation," *American Journal of Sociology*, Vol. LXIV, No. 4, January, 1959, pp. 364–374.

index of segregation equivalent to the percentage of the particular minority group which would have to relocate to effect an even, unsegregated population distribution. Their index indicated that 28 per cent of the foreign-born whites (from early immigrations) and 41 per cent of the foreign-born whites (from relatively more recent immigrations) would have to move in order to match the distribution of native whites.

By contrast, the index of segregation for Negroes in relation to various groups of foreign-born whites ranged from 79 to 94 per cent. In relation to native whites, 85 per cent of the Negroes in the city would have had to move in 1930 to balance the distribution.

In a later study of ten cities, using a similar index, Lieberson[19] found that segregation of foreign-born whites had been dramatically *reduced* over the twenty-year period from 1930 to 1950. Again, by contrast, Negro segregation in relation to native whites had *increased* in eight of the ten cities. In relation to foreign-born whites, it had increased in nine of the ten.

In 1960, the Taeubers conducted a study of 207 cities, using essentially the same segregation index.[20] The average index of Negro segregation from all the cities was 86 per cent, with regional variations ranging from an index of 76 per cent in New England to 91 per cent in the South Atlantic states. This and other data prompted the Taeubers to conclude:

... comparing the residential segregation of various ethnic and minority groups from each other and from whites, has demonstrated that current levels of Negro-white segregation are higher than those between any nationality group and native whites.[21]

Thus, the Negro migration—in effect, an internal immigration of vast proportions—had a significant impact upon the North and West and South. But it had a similarly significant impact upon the Negro himself. As Hauser concludes:

... between 1910 and 1960, the Negro has been redistributed from the South to the North and West, and from rural to urban and metropoli-

---

[19] Stanley Lieberson, "The Impact of Residential Segregation and Ethnic Assimilation," *Social Forces*, Vol. 40, No. 1, October, 1961, pp. 52–57.
[20] Karl E. Taeuber and Alma F. Taeuber, *Negroes in Cities* (Chicago: Aldine Publishing Company, 1965), pp. 36–37. Copyright © 1965 by Karl E. and Alma F. Taeuber.
[21] *Ibid.*, p. 34.

tan areas; but within the urban and metropolitan complexes the Negro American has become and has remained much more highly segregated than was true of white immigrants who flocked to the cities before them.[22]

While Negroes have been migrating to the cities, whites have been leaving the cities for the surrounding suburbs at an unprecedented rate. The result of this dual trend is that we are rapidly creating two cities within metropolitan areas—a black core, and a white ring.

All fifty of the largest cities in the United States showed an increase in the percentage of non-whites between 1950 and 1960. But this trend is not restricted to the largest American cities. For example, Flint, Grand Rapids, Pontiac, and Muskegon, Michigan, which rank 62, 71, 171, 335 in size of U.S. cities, all doubled their Negro populations between 1950 and 1960. Negroes first migrated to the largest cities, but now are branching out to much smaller cities in search of jobs and opportunity. In almost every case, they are inheriting a deteriorated inner core as whites flee to the suburbs.

Table 3 shows the shocking reality of this population redistribution in the thirty largest U. S. cities.[23] Moreover, there seems to be no evidence that this trend will reverse itself any time in the immediate future. Washington, D. C. was 54 per cent Negro in 1960, the first major city to have a majority of Negro citizens. This "blackening" of the central city has continued at an unprecedented rate, and in 1965 it was estimated that 66 per cent of the Washington, D. C. population was Negro. It is not at all clear *when* or even *if* this redistribution of Negro and white population will stabilize. It is possible that cities may go the same route as so many neighborhoods have—once they reach a tipping point, they may become nearly all black.

Newark, New Jersey has gone the same route as Washington, D. C. In 1950 only 17 per cent of the city's population was Negro. This percentage doubled to 34 per cent by 1960 and the Bureau of the Census estimated that Newark was 47 per cent Negro in 1965.

[22] Hauser, *op. cit.*, p. 77.
[23] U. S. Department of Labor, Bureau of Labor Statistics, *Social and Economic Conditions of Negroes in the United States* (Washington, D. C.: Government Printing Office, 1967), p. 11.

TABLE 3

PERACENTAGE OF NEGROES IN EACH OF THE 30 LARGEST CITIES,
1950, 1960, AND ESTIMATED 1965

	1950	1960	(Estimate) 1965
New York, N. Y.	10	14	18
Chicago, Ill.	14	23	28
Los Angeles, Calif.	9	14	17
Philadelphia, Pa.	18	26	31
Detroit, Mich.	16	29	34
Baltimore, Md.	24	35	38
Houston, Tex.	21	23	23
Cleveland, Ohio	16	29	34
Washington, D. C.	35	54	66
St. Louis, Mo.	18	29	36
Milwaukee, Wis.	3	8	11
San Francisco, Calif.	6	10	12
Boston, Mass.	5	9	13
Dallas, Tex.	13	19	21
New Orleans, La.	32	37	41
Pittsburgh, Pa.	12	17	20
San Antonio, Tex.	7	7	8
San Diego, Calif.	5	6	7
Seattle, Wash.	3	5	7
Buffalo, N. Y.	6	13	17
Cincinnati, Ohio	16	22	24
Memphis, Tenn.	37	37	40
Denver, Colo.	4	6	9
Atlanta, Ga.	37	38	44
Minneapolis, Minn.	1	2	4
Indianapolis, Ind.	15	21	23
Kansas City, Mo.	12	18	22
Columbus, Ohio	12	16	18
Phoenix, Ariz.	5	5	5
Newark, N. J.	17	34	47

A study by Rutgers University in 1967 showed that the Negro population in Newark had increased 52 per cent.[24] An additional 10 per cent was classified as "other nonwhite"—mostly Spanish speaking.

[24] Cited in: Governor's Select Commission on Civil Disorder, *Report for Action* (state of New Jersey, February, 1968), p. 2.

Other major cities are almost certain to go the same route. The President's Commission on Civil Disorders predicted that eleven additional major cities will have a majority Negro population by 1984. These cities and the dates when they are estimated to have a 50 per cent Negro population are listed in Table 4.

TABLE 4

PREDICTED DATE OF 50% NEGRO POPULATION
IN CENTRAL CITIES

New Orleans, La.	1971
Richmond, Va.	1971
Baltimore, Md.	1972
Jacksonville, Fla.	1972
Gary, Ind.	1973
Cleveland, Ohio	1975
St. Louis, Mo.	1978
Detroit, Mich.	1979
Philadelphia, Pa.	1981
Oakland, Calif.	1983
Chicago, Ill.	1984[25]

If the commission's projections are correct, seven of the ten largest U.S. cities will have a majority Negro population within the next fifteen years. But there is reason to believe these cities as well as others may reach a tipping point well ahead of these projections. Many local observers, for example, feel that Cleveland and Gary may have Negro majorities by 1970—largely as the result of accelerated white exodus caused by election of Negro mayors in November, 1967.

These figures are not only a slap in the face to the goal of creating an integrated society, they also sound a warning of impending financial disaster for our large central cities, for as we will see in more detail shortly, the economic advancement of the Negro is not progressing rapidly enough so that they can hope to assume responsibility for rehabilitating the central city cores that are already badly suffering from neglect.

Before turning to the status of the Negro in America today,

---

[25] Report of the National Advisory Commission on Civil Disorders (Washington, D. C.: Government Printing Office, 1968), p. 216.

a final area of demography needs to be examined. While many Negroes migrated North and West, many remained in the South. The urbanization trend in the South has not been as rapid as in other regions of the country.[26] In 1960, only 58 per cent of southern Negroes and 59 per cent of southern whites lived in urban areas (2,500 or greater population). Using this same criterion to define an urban population, nearly all Negroes in the North live in cities—96 per cent, compared with only 75 per cent of all whites. The same distribution pattern is repeated in the West where 93 per cent of the Negro population is urbanized, while 78 per cent of the white population is so concentrated. In the South, Negroes and whites have traditionally shared similar urban-rural concentrations. However, as Negroes migrated North and West, they bypassed the rural areas and concentrated almost exclusively in cities.

In the older cities of the South, the Negro population is somewhat more scattered than in the North. Small Negro settlements do exist, but there are generally many of them, spread throughout the city. Frazier was one of the first to note and analyze this seeming anomaly:

In the older cities, like Charleston, with a large Negro population, the Negroes are widely scattered. The location of the widely scattered Negro population is due largely to historical factors. Small Negro settlements, comprised mostly of servants, have grown up close to the houses of the whites in which the Negroes served. These settlements thus took root before the spatial pattern of the cities was affected by the economic forces which have shaped the pattern of our modern industrial and commercial cities.[27]

But once the cities in the South begin to develop along the lines of the major industrial complexes of the urban North, the same pattern of racial segregation apparent in the North begin to appear:

The second general pattern appears in the newer cities of the South, or in cities where industry and commerce have determined their spatial pattern. In these latter cities, there are several large concentrations of Negroes and the remainder of the Negro population is

[26] Taeuber and Taeuber, "The Negro Population in the United States," *op. cit.*, p. 118.
[27] Frazier, *op. cit.*, p. 237.

scattered lightly over a large area. The light scattering of Negroes over a large area is attributable ... to historical factors, while the large concentrations of the Negro population reflect the increasing influence of economic and social forces inherent in the growth of the modern city.[28]

The Taeubers note the same pattern in their studies. They state that the differences in Southern cities between "light scattering" and the "large concentrations" are due mainly to whether the city grew up before or after the Civil War.[29] In the older cities, the intermixture is more likely. In the newer cities, the segregation pattern is more likely. Their explanation of the historical differentiation attributes the divergent situations to the presence of large ante-bellum groups of free Negroes in the older cities. Negroes in the older cities had already established scattered pockets and later arrivals simply added to their numbers.[30]

So, while the freed Negro clustered in scattered, well-established pockets in the older cities, he moved into the newer cities as a relative stranger. In the newer cities, his arrival and location resulted in patterns of segregation similar to those encountered by his peer moving northward. Since the cities were new, there were no 'domestic' Negro pockets around which to cluster, so the Negro entered the newer cities without a pre-established relationship giving him claim to territory near whites.

When the growth of Negro population was large enough, however, even the older cities established patterns of segregation similar to those in the North. Note the Taeubers:

The residential intermingling characteristic of the older cities before the War diminished gradually in succeeding decades, and the relative importance of these older areas in the total housing picture depends upon the rate of post-Civil War growth in Negro population.[31]

Cities like Atlanta, Birmingham, and Memphis, despite some Negro in-migration, still have a degree of 'scattering.' But cities like Baltimore and Washington exhibit greater concentrations. Thus, as the South increases its urbanization, it is likely to increase the process of ghettoizing its black residents.

[28] *Ibid.*
[29] Taeuber and Taeuber, *op. cit.,* p. 190.
[30] *Ibid.*
[31] *Ibid.,* p. 192.

THE NEGRO TODAY

In sixteenth century Venice, Jews were clustered in a section of the city known as a ghetto. As the decades passed, any section of a city to which Jews were confined was given the name. In America, as the term is now used, a ghetto constitutes a restricted area reserved for persons of a particular ethnic or racial background. Every minority group in America has been or is currently confined to a ghetto. As the Negro became urbanized, he too was ghettoized, but to a greater degree and for a far longer time than other minorities.

While the sixteenth century Venetian ghetto was not necessarily a haven for only the poverty-stricken, the American ghetto is—and particularly the American Negro ghetto. Residents of such ghettoes are second-class citizens in the worst sense of the term. If they have jobs, they tend to be the most menial in terms of quality and pay. Living conditions tend to be squalid; family structures unstable; traditional morality irrelevant; and crime rates high. As Kenneth Clark eloquently summarizes:

> The objective dimensions of the American urban ghettos are overcrowded and deteriorated housing, high infant mortality, crime, and disease. The subjective dimensions are resentment, hostility, despair, apathy, self-depreciation, and its ironic companion, compensatory grandiose behavior.[32]

These conditions are commonly recognized by those aware of the ghetto's existence—those who live there, those who exploit its inhabitants, and those who by chance cannot avoid its physical presence. But most Americans are still not aware of the degree of misery that the ghetto condition assures for its inhabitants.

As the Negro's drive for *de jure* equality gained momentum, exposures of ghetto conditions appeared, painting dire pictures of the segregated islands which pockmark the otherwise plentiful landscape with their masses living in almost sub-human existence. Books such as Harrington's *The Other America*[33] should have meant that the nation could no longer avoid recognition of the continued presence of its cancerous injustices. But Americans have

[32] Kenneth B. Clark, *The Dark Ghetto* (New York: Harper & Row, Publishers, 1965), p. 11.
[33] Michael Harrington, *The Other America: Poverty in the United States* (New York: The Macmillan Company, 1963).

a peculiar ability to become quickly disturbed by a disquieting situation and to be just as quickly anesthetized to the deep-rooted causes and meanings of their perturbation.

This is not to say, of course, that short-term responses to the Negro's demand for progress did not occur. The war on poverty was begun in 1964. President Johnson had promised a full-scale assault on our nation's social problems, an assault which would result in a Great Society. The goal set for the sixties seemed to be that of eliminating the material problems which plagued our progress and diverted our attention from higher pursuits. Once the material problems of food, shelter, and health had been conquered for all our citizens, we could go on to pursue an American dream of one sort or another.

Gradually, the nation developed its ill-founded complacency. Just as in the past, when muckrakers had created their stir and achieved some of their noble longings, the nation settled back— somewhat disturbed, to be sure, by the first rumblings of ghetto violence—with the satisfaction that the government programs for the ghetto would mollify any pangs of conscience that white America might feel. This satisfaction, coupled with the preliminary reports of success in the government's war on poverty, developed an expectation throughout white America that all these efforts had to be making a difference for the Negro, a difference which he should recognize and appreciate. Legislation, judicial decision, and administrative action had indeed all operated to grant the Negro his legal rights. And the war on poverty was there to translate these rights into meaningful results. Surely the barriers of prejudice which blocked the Negro's road to progress for a century since Emancipation had crumbled through the determined efforts of a society enlightened in its attitudes toward the Negro condition and committed to an improvement of that condition.

Despite the riots of the sixties which have thus far occurred, white America still finds it hard to believe that its assumption of steady progress for the Negro is an unreal supposition. White America still implicitly believes that progress is being made on the Negro 'problem.' After four summers of racial violence, *Fortune* published the following interpretation:

There is so much authentic bad news about the condition of American Negroes these days, and so much guilt about the bad news among

American whites, that it is often hard to get a hearing for some re-
markable good news. Much of it is in the form of government data ...
Negroes have been steadily moving out of the slums ... By several
other indicators, furthermore, the gap between Negroes and whites is
being narrowed; and by just about all indicators, Negroes are far
better off today than they were in the recent past.[34]

The author of this conclusion has failed to do only one thing,
to honor a *caveat* of the ghetto and the hip: He has failed to
"tell it like it is!" Like the vast majority of white America, he
is unwilling to admit that the current efforts have failed to produce really *meaningful* progress for the masses of American Negroes. Such progress has not been achieved, nor is it likely to be
in the near future. After the inauguration of the poverty program,
after significant legislation, expenditures, and efforts, even after
some gains had been registered, urbanologist Daniel P. Moynihan
could write:

> The United States is approaching a new crisis in race relations ...
> In this new period the expectations of the Negro Americans will go
> beyond civil rights. Being Americans, they will now expect that in the
> near future equal opportunities for them as a group will produce
> roughly equal results, as compared with other groups. This is not
> going to happen. Nor will it happen for generations to come unless a
> new and special effort is made ...
> The most difficult fact for white Americans to understand is that
> ... the circumstances of the Negro American community in recent
> years have been getting *worse, not better*.[35]

That was in March of 1965. In September of 1967, Moynihan
implied before a nationwide television audience that, from his
perspective, the picture had not changed.[36] In 1965, Moynihan was
scathingly criticized by some as a cynical and skeptical prophet
of doom. In 1967 there were still many unwilling to remember that
Cassandra had been right.

Perhaps tokenism as a term has been overworked, but as a fact

---

[34] Edmund K. Faltermayer, "More Dollars and More Diplomas," *Fortune*, January, 1968, p. 140. Courtesy of *Fortune* Magazine, January 1968
Issue; © 1968, Time, Inc.

[35] U. S. Department of Labor, Office of Policy Planning and Research,
The Negro Family: The Case for National Action (Washington, D. C.:
Government Printing Office, 1965), p. i.

[36] Based on remarks of Daniel P. Moynihan on N.B.C., September 15,
1967.

of life for the masses of Negroes it is only too applicable. Some gains, some achievements have been made. But no significant progress toward improving the everyday lives of the ghettoized masses has been registered. In fact, those everyday lives may be slightly worse than they were, say, a decade ago, despite the thriving status of the other half of "The Other America."

The hard underlying realization America must come to is that the ghetto has neither disappeared nor materially improved. If anything, the problem of segregation and the resultant misery of the ghetto have increased in our major urban areas.

Cleveland, Ohio, is the only city in the nation to have a city-wide census conducted since the decennial tally of 1960. In 1965, the U.S. Bureau of the Census conducted a special census in Cleveland to test some new measurement techniques.[37] A hard look at the Cleveland data challenges our wide spread desire to believe that conditions are improving in leaps and bounds.

Before turning to the Cleveland data, let us remind ourselves of the optimism of the *Fortune* writer:

In 1960 some 139,000 Negroes lived in Hough and the three other communities that make up Cleveland's bad slums; five years later the Negro population had dwindled to 119,000 even though the total Negro population of Cleveland had increased from 251,000 to 276,000. "Today," says a federal economist who has closely analyzed the data, "most Negro families no longer live in slums, they simply live in Negro neighborhoods."[38]

The most striking demographic feature of Cleveland is its population redistribution.[39] The metropolitan area has a population of something less than two million residents, but more than half of these persons reside outside of the central city. Between 1950 and

[37] Data for the special 1965 Cleveland census appear in several reports: U. S. Department of Commerce, Bureau of the Census, *Special Census of Cleveland, Ohio, April 1, 1965*, Series P-28, No. 1390; *Changes in Economic Level in Nine Neighborhoods in Cleveland: 1960–1965*, Series P-23, No. 20; and *Characteristics of Selected Neighborhoods in Cleveland, Ohio: April 1965*, Series P-23, No. 21 (Washington, D. C.: Government Printing Office, 1965, 1966, 1967).

[38] Faltermayer, *op. cit.*, p. 222.

[39] For a more detailed discussion of background data on Cleveland see: Jeffrey K. Hadden, Louis H. Masotti, and Victor Thiessen, "The Making of the Negro Mayors 1967," *Trans-Action*, January–February, 1968, pp. 21–30.

1960, the population of the central city declined from 914,808 to 876,050, a loss of almost 39,000. By 1965 the population had dropped to 810,858, an additional 65,000 loss. But these figures only partially reflect the changing population composition, since new Negro residents coming into the central city partially offset the white exodus. *Between 1950 and 1960, nearly 142,000 white residents left the central city, and an additional 94,000 left between 1960 and 1965—nearly a quarter of a million in just fifteen years!*

During the same period, the number of Negro residents of Cleveland rose from 147,847 to 279,352—an increase from 16.1 to 34.4 per cent of the city's population. In 1960, approximately 97 per cent of the Negroes in the metropolitan area lived in the central city. Some suburbanization of Negroes had occurred since 1960, but the pace has not been nearly so dramatic as for whites. Much of the Negro 'suburbanization' that has taken place is into East Cleveland—an older decaying residential area that is only an extension of Cleveland's east side ghetto.

In 1960, the city had twenty-seven census tracts with Negro populations of 90 per cent or more. These twenty-seven tracts contained 134,142 (53.5%) of the city's 250,818 Negroes. The 1965 census indicates that the number of tracts with 90 per cent plus Negro inhabitants had increased from twenty-seven to thirty-nine. These thirty-nine tracts now held 180,372 (64.6%) of the city's 279,352 non-whites. Thus, in both absolute and relative terms, Negroes were growing in numbers and in concentrations in the dark ghetto.

The implicit assumption of the *Fortune* article is that Negroes are becoming more affluent and moving out of the slums. The data in the above paragraph which demonstrate increasing concentration of Negroes, while shattering the myth of increasing integration, do not necessarily contradict the *Fortune* assertion that most Negroes no longer live in slums, but only Negro neighborhoods. What, in fact, has happened to the Negro in Cleveland?

The answer depends in part on how one chooses to look at the data. The Bureau of the Census selected six predominantly Negro neighborhoods for special analysis. Five of these neighborhoods have been designated by the Office of Economic Opportunity as poverty areas. The sixth is in a state of transition and various groups wanted to take a closer look at what is happening in the neighborhood. A special census report presented detailed comparisons of these six neighborhoods with Negroes in the rest of the city.

To a nation that is obsessed with finding signs of hope, the results can be read with hope and optimism. For example, the number of Negroes living outside of these six areas nearly *doubled* between 1960 and 1965. The proportion of Negro families outside this area which were below poverty level standards dropped from 17.9 to 9.8 per cent. The figures for Negro families with female heads who are below poverty level are even more encouraging: 25 per cent in 1965 compared with 53.5 per cent in 1960. Improvement in income levels also looks good. In 1960, the median income for Negro families living outside the six predominantly black neighborhoods was $6,178. By 1965 this figure rose to $7,285—a gain of $1,100.

But this is a distorted picture. *Eighty-five per cent of Cleveland's Negroes live within the six predominately black neighborhoods!* Moreover, this represents a population increase of 2.9 per cent over 1960. For this large majority, the change between 1960 and 1965 was not nearly so dramatic. Most of the 235,000 residents of these six neighborhoods barely managed to stay even with their condition in 1960 or else fell even further behind. The percentage of families below poverty level increased by 2.4. Households with female heads who are below poverty level rose from 58.1 to 63.5 per cent. The median family income for the six areas rose only $132, from $4,953 in 1960 to $5,085 in 1965. And this is largely a function of the two more 'affluent' neighborhoods. Four of the six neighborhoods experienced a decline in income. These four neighborhoods, representing approximately 40 per cent of the total Negro population in Cleveland, had a median family income of only $3,600. The average income for Cleveland residents outside of the designated poverty areas in 1965 was $7,642. (Average incomes are even higher in almost all of the surrounding suburban communities.)

Thus, the objective economic condition of the large majority of Cleveland Negroes is either declining or falling behind relative to the rest of the metropolitan area. Our point is not to ignore *some* significant gains that have been made by *some* Negroes. But to focus our attention on this group is to ignore the objective reality of the majority—a reality which is growing increasingly impatient and bitter in a world of increasing affluency for most and a world of rising expectations for nearly all.

A special survey census conducted in Watts in 1965 uncovered information similar to the Cleveland census.[40] The number of families in Watts below poverty level dropped just one per cent (from 44% to 43%) between 1960 and 1965. Median income rose just $139 while much more substantial gains were being made in all white neighborhoods of Los Angeles. The proportion of housing units that were classified as deteriorating or dilapidated rose from 16 to 25 per cent, etc.

Cleveland and Watts are two areas that have been rocked with violence and unrest. How typical are they of Negro neighborhoods across the country? Again, the answer has to be somewhat subjective and depends on what statistics are examined and how they are interpreted. But the answer is that they are more typical than we would like to believe.

The most comprehensive and recent body of data on American Negroes is found in a joint publication of the Bureau of Labor statistics and the Bureau of the Census, October, 1967 entitled *Social and Economic Conditions of Negroes in the United States.* The report has a somewhat biased interpretation of the statistics— in part because, as we have stressed above, white society wants to believe that things are getting better, but also because the federal government has a vested interest in demonstrating that its programs to eliminate poverty are working. Nevertheless, the writers of the report cannot escape the ambiguity and tenuousness of the progress that has been made. They conclude:

The statistics provide a mixed picture. There are signs of great improvement in some sections and of deterioration in others. The data show that large numbers of Negroes are for the first time in American history entering into the middle-income bracket and into better environments in which to raise their families.

Yet others remain trapped in the poverty of the slums, their living conditions either unchanged or deteriorating.

The kaleidoscopic pattern begins to make sense only when we stop

[40] U. S. Department of Labor, *Social and Economic Conditions of Negroes in the United States, op. cit.,* p. 96. For a more detailed description of demographic characteristics of Watts see: U. S. Department of Commerce, Bureau of the Census, *Characteristics of the South and East Los Angeles Areas November 1965,* Series P-23, No. 18. (Washington, D. C.: Government Printing Office, 1966).

thinking of the Negro as a homogeneous, undifferentiated group and begin to think of Negroes as individuals who differ widely in their aspirations, abilities, experiences and opportunities ...

This complicated pattern of progress mixed with some retrogression makes it hazardous to generalize about the social and economic conditions of Negroes in America. The statistics show dramatic achievements; they also reveal a large remaining gap between the circumstances of whites and Negroes.[41]

Earlier in this volume we noted the fallacy that most white Americans engage in when they look at the Negro community as a homogeneous whole. Such generalizing was seen to be valid in determining the Negro's mood. Once again, we would stress that it is impossible to accurately analyze the Negro's objective position in American society by looking at him in overall statistics. Nor, because part of the Negro community is making improvements in wages and housing, can we conclude that the situation of the masses of Negroes in American slum-ghettos is significantly improving. For, in fact, when we carefully dissect the data, it becomes painfully clear that only a small proportion of America's Negroes are making any significant strides toward economic and social equality.

The government report on the social and economic condition of Negroes warns against this fallacy of lumping all Negroes together. Yet, almost all the data they present does just this. And even having done so, they still must conclude that the gains are tenuous. Take, for example, the trends in unemployment presented in Table 5. Between 1958 and 1967, non-white unemployment fell from 12.6 to 7.3 per cent—clearly a significant drop. During the same period of time white unemployment dropped from 6.1 to 3.4 per cent. The ratio of non-white to white unemployment remained unchanged. In fact, during the early 1950's the ratio of non-white to white unemployment was even lower.

Quite obviously, unemployment figures do not tell the whole story, just as any other single statistic does not tell the whole story. But to unfold the story more adequately is to show more clearly the disadvantaged position of the Negro. Unemployment is higher in younger age groups—Negro and white—but the Negro's situation is considerably more acute. Among teenagers (16–19 years

[41] *Ibid.*, pp. VII–VIII.

TABLE 5

UNEMPLOYMENT RATES,* 1949–1967

	Non-white	White	Ratio non-white to white
1949	8.9	5.6	1.6
1950	9.0	4.9	1.8
1951	5.3	3.1	1.7
1952	5.4	2.8	1.9
1953	4.5	2.7	1.7
1954	9.9	5.0	2.0
1955	8.7	3.9	2.2
1956	8.3	3.6	2.3
1957	7.9	3.8	2.1
1958	12.6	6.1	2.1
1959	10.7	4.8	2.2
1960	10.2	4.9	2.1
1961	12.4	6.0	2.1
1962	10.9	4.9	2.2
1963	10.8	5.0	2.2
1964	9.6	4.6	2.1
1965	8.1	4.1	2.0
1966	7.3	3.3	2.2
1967 (*First 9 months seasonally adjusted*)	7.3	3.4	2.1[42]

* *The unemployment rate is the percentage unemployed in the civilian labor force.*

old) who are in the job market (i.e., looking for work), 26.5 per cent of the Negroes are unemployed compared with 10.6 per cent of the whites.

The statistical system of the Department of Labor determines unemployment rates as a percentage of those who are actively seeking jobs over all those in the labor force. Those not seeking jobs, for whatever reason, are not counted as unemployed. In non-poverty areas, the proportion of men in prime working ages (21–54) who are not members of the labor force was two and one half per cent. In poverty areas, the proportion of whites not in the labor force was three and one half per cent. But for Negro poverty areas, the proportion was eight per cent. The majority of these Negroes

[42] *Ibid.*, p. 30.

reported illness or disability as the main reason for non-participation. Wetzel and Holland doubt the validity of this claim:

> The high incidence of disability reported for Negro men in the central ages deserves further study. Undoubtedly, disability rates are higher for these men; however, if an adult male in the family is not working or seeking work, the respondent to a household survey may find it easier and more acceptable to say that he is unable to work. Preliminary evidence also suggests that psychosomatic illness associated with discouragement contributed to this rate.[43]

But the unemployed and those who are not in the labor market do not complete the list of disadvantaged Negroes. The 1960 census missed approximately ten per cent of the Negro population. What reason is there to believe that sample surveys conducted by the Bureau of Labor Statistics do not miss a similar proportion of Negroes—transient, poor, and jobless? Moreover, inadequate statistics are not available on underemployment. The *Manpower Report of the President* estimated that about two million workers were employed only part time during an average week in 1966, and Negroes are disproportionately affected by part time employment.[44]

Such statistics, no matter how complete or detailed, cannot tell the whole story, but they do help to piece together a picture of how the Negro is faring in the marketplace. And the more closely the statistics are examined, the clearer it becomes that he is faring badly.

While a small proportion of Negroes are making significant gains, the truth is that the large majority of Negroes are becoming increasingly *irrelevant* to the economy of this country. Willhelm and Powell argue forcefully that the struggle between black and white for equality is too narrow in scope. They see the growing crisis as being caused "not so much by the transition from slavery to equality as by a change from an economics of exploitation to an economics of uselessness."[45]

[43] James R. Wetzel and Susan S. Holland, "Poverty Areas of Our Major Cities," *Monthly Labor Review*, October, 1966, p. 1109.

[44] U. S. Department of Labor, *Manpower Report of the President,* Transmitted to the Congress April, 1967, (Washington, D. C.: Government Printing Office, 1967), p. 126.

[45] Sidney M. Willhelm and Edwin H. Powell, "Who Needs the Negro?," *Trans-Action*, September–October, 1964, p. 3.

They proceed to argue that:

The tremendous historical change for the Negro is taking place in these terms: he is not needed. He is not so much oppressed as unwanted; not so much unwanted as unnecessary; not so much abused as ignored. The dominant whites no longer need to exploit him. If he disappeared tomorrow he would hardly be missed. As automation proceeds, it is easier and easier to disregard him.[46]

This is a harsh and frightening argument, but the discord it rings has a certain truth and shocking reality that will not let us dismiss it—job training programs that teach skills for which there are no jobs on antique machinery that was long ago discarded by industry . . . summer jobs that are not jobs at all, but payoffs to 'cool it' . . . welfare programs which perpetuate poverty . . . declaration of war on poverty with a token budget and a token army without leadership or a strategy to win.

Perhaps our token efforts are only a way of deceiving ourselves and avoiding facing up to the fact that we wish the Negro would go away. But he will not go away, and in increasing numbers he is coming to understanding how it really is.

The black man is still being deprived of his right to share in the abundance of an economy that is in a period of unabated expansion. He is still deprived of his right to be a man, even as we approach the 200th birthday of a nation founded to guarantee that right above all. Some have given up all hope. Others are reaching new depths of frustration and bitterness. They no longer ask to be heard. They demand it. The burning and looting of the past four summers cannot be understood in any other terms. It is as primitive a form of communication as is known to man. And still we don't hear, or if we do, we misunderstand.

The 'problem' referred to by W. E. B. DuBois is not a Negro problem. It is a problem that cuts as deep as the very meaning and purpose of this nation. We must face this problem squarely or all that has gone before will become irrelevant. The tragedy of the Negro is a tragedy of America itself. Unless we can end this continuing tragedy, no man in this nation shall be free.

[46] *Ibid.*

chapter five

RACIAL VIOLENCE
IN AMERICAN HISTORY

Racial violence, wreaking havoc and terror in literally dozens of American cities over the last several years, has surprised and shocked many Americans. In their concern with the immediate crisis facing the nation, they lose sight of the reality that violence is a long-standing tradition of the American way of life.

On July 29, 1967, in the midst of the worst summer of violence in the current wave, President Johnson appointed a blue-ribbon commission to answer three questions:

What happened?

Why did it happen?

What could be done to prevent it from happening again?[1]

The questions indicate a strong and justified concern for the immediate. However, the very nature of the questions seems to imply that the current violence is somehow a new phenomenon. In fact, racial violence is and has been a dominant theme in the relations between Negroes and whites in American history. From the days of the burgeoning slave trade to the present, violence has at least been a threat—and often a gruesomely poignant reality— in interracial affairs. Thus, the attempt to unravel the 'mystery' of the current violence must deal with the violence of the past. In no other way can the forces involved in determining the nature of the present violence be understood.

[1] *New York Times*, July 30, 1967.

Perhaps the President was correct in assuming that the nation knew almost nothing about the nature of the current wave of violence. If so, it was not because violence was new or because some analysis of violence was not available. Rather, it was because until 1964 the horror of civil violence did not constitute a crisis pressing upon the consciousness of the current generation. This, despite the continuing tradition of violence in this country which sociologist Allen Grimshaw describes:

America has been then, a land of lawlessness and violence, ranging from spontaneous brawls between servicemen of different branches and schoolboys of different schools, through the 'blood feud' and gangster warfare, to the full-fledged military campaigns which have occurred in struggles between class and class and between adherents of different religious faiths. The tradition of lawlessness includes both a contempt of parking regulations and an admiration of gangster heroes and, on the other hand, an excess zeal in the administration of 'vigilante justice,' 'lynch law,' and 'six-shooter law' on the frontier.[2]

The purpose of this chapter is to trace and explain the patterns of violence, evolved over the decades, between Negroes and whites in the United States. The violent events cited below are intended to be illustrative of the types of violence which have occurred and of the times at which they appeared.

SUPPRESSION AND INSURRECTION

One of the inherent assumptions of slavery was the necessity of violence. A white master maintained complete dominance over his slaves through his monopoly of the instruments of violence. Physical force was an inherent part of the system of slavery. Neither law nor informal patterns of conduct placed restrictions on the slave master's use of violence. In fact, white neighbors and local police were available to assist in the control and suppression of slaves.

It is easy to understand why violence was rampant in the slave system when we examine the unique context of slavery in America. The institution of slavery has obviously contradicted the claims of

[2] Allen D. Grimshaw, *A Study in Social Violence: Urban Race Riots in the United States* (unpublished doctoral dissertation, University of Pennsylvania, 1959), p. 20.

American society that democracy meant freedom for all. Only the assumption that Negroes were not part of the "all"—i.e., that they were somehow inferior—could justify the slave system.

The Negro did pose a dilemma. The citizens of this new land had been deeply influenced by the emerging ideology of constitutional government which stressed the rights of men rather than the rights of those who govern. Indeed, John Locke had argued that the social contract must exist among free men. How could this ideology prevail in a society which also embraced slavery? The only possible argument to justify such an inconsistency revolved around the consideration of the Negro as inherently inferior. And, indeed, this is the ideology that emerged. Negroes were not quite men. As such, they lacked the capacity to be free men. The system of slavery, thus, in no way denied rights to those capable of possessing such rights—white men.

With this justification at hand, a master was free to do with his slaves as he wished. Much of the South's economy became focused upon and, later, captured by this institutional arrangement in which master totally dominated slave in every aspect of the latter's existence—work, religion, sex, political behavior, etc. The lives of the slaves were closely controlled as their energies were exploited in the interest of their masters. With the slave considered an inferior creature, violence or the threat of violence necessarily became the mechanism whereby the domination and regulation of the slaves' lives could be maintained.

Negro reaction to the slave condition also involved violence. Slave revolts, though hardly ever successful in any meaningful sense, were feared by whites and are important to our consideration of the patterns of violence permeating Negro-white relations in America. Such revolts represented an attempt on the part of the Negroes to attack the system suppressing them by destroying the source of their oppression. Thus, they were aimed at killing whites.

One of the first slave insurrections of major consequence occurred in Virginia in 1800.[3] Leading the well-planned revolt was

[3] For a more complete discussion of this revolt and the others mentioned here, see: E. Franklin Frazier, *The Negro in the United States* (New York: The Macmillan Company, 1949), pp. 87–93; Benjamin Brawley, *A Social History of the American Negro* (New York: The Mac-

a young Negro slave named Gabriel, who developed his mechanism of revolt during the summer of 1800 through a series of meetings with other slaves. At the meetings, Gabriel's brother Martin interpreted various passages of Scripture to inspire the other slaves to revolt. Available information indicates that several of the passages referred to the Israelites casting off their yoke of oppression. Thus, believing that God would come to their aid, a force of 1,100 Negroes was scheduled to gather at a spot about six miles from Richmond. Gabriel's plan was to march on the city of 8,000 in three columns. The right wing would seize the penitentiary building, recently converted into an arsenal. The left wing would take possession of the powderhouse. Meanwhile, the third column, and major wing, would begin the slaughter armed only with a few muskets, knives, and pikes. After the arsenal and powderhouse contents were in hand, the marauders would be well enough armed to easily conquer the 400–500 men in Richmond (who had only 30 additional muskets among them).

On the day appointed for the uprising, a damaging storm struck Virginia. Bridges were washed out, roads and plantations were completely submerged, and Brook Swamp—the strategic meeting point for the slave rebels—became totally inundated. Much of Gabriel's band could not even travel to get to their assembly point. Only 300 of the expected 1,100 rebels appeared at the designated hour. Overcome by fear and superstition, the tiny group disbanded without even an attempt at revolt.

Gabriel's misfortunes had only begun, however, since at least one, and perhaps several, of his fellow slaves revealed the plot to their masters. (It must be remembered, in this regard, that some slaves were so ingrained with the system of slavery that they accepted the explanation of their own inferiority, liked the system, or simply didn't wish to create controversy; therefore, they protected and obeyed their masters with often fierce loyalty.)

All Richmond was soon in arms, a cavalry troop was ordered into the city, and numerous arrests of suspected conspirators en-

---

millan Company, 1921), pp. 86–90, 132–148; Allen Grimshaw, "Lawlessness and Violence in America and Their Special Manifestations in Changing Negro-White Relationships," *Journal of Negro History*, Vol. XLIV, January, 1959, p. 52ff; Harvey Wish, "American Slave Insurrections Before 1861," *Journal of Negro History*, Vol. XXII, July, 1937, pp. 299–320.

sued. Six were convicted and executed on September 12. Five more were executed on September 18 and Gabriel himself was executed October 7. Twenty-four more conspirators were executed later.

The Governor of Virginia entered into a secret correspondence with President Jefferson in hopes of securing a grant of land to which troublesome slaves could be banished. A secret session of the Virginia legislature met in 1805 and passed a resolution embodying the Governor's proposal. No action resulted, however, either from the plea to the President or from the legislative resolution.

It is important to note that Gabriel's activities took the form of an anti-white revolution: the slaves involved had planned to slaughter all the residents of Richmond with the exception of the French. (The slaves identified their own aspirations as being in concert with those of the French Revolution.)

The second slave uprising of major consequence was elaborately staged by Denmark Vesey in Charleston, South Carolina, in 1822. He was one of three hundred and ninety slaves brought on the ship of Captain Vesey to be sold at Cape Francois, Santo Domingo. Here, Denmark was purchased by a wealthy plantation owner. On his next trip to Santo Domingo, however, Vesey learned that Denmark was to be returned to him as physically unsound and subject to epileptic fits. Denmark served Captain Vesey as personal attendant until 1800. In this year, he, now 33 years of age and living in Charleston, won a lottery prize of $1,500. With $600 of this sum, Denmark purchased his freedom.

Denmark Vesey's high level of intelligence was demonstrated by his fluency in both French and English; he read extensively and seems to have been acquainted with the successful slave uprisings in Haiti, the principles of the French Revolution, and the debates over the Missouri Compromise. Vesey used his mastery of such topics to convince other Negroes to join his movement. Carefully planning his activities, Vesey waited until 1820 before beginning active recruitment for his proposed insurrection. He discreetly chose four lieutenants, each of whom kept careful accounts of recruits in code.

Sunday, July 14, 1822, was the date set for attack. The month had been chosen strategically, because Vesey realized that many whites and their families would be away at resorts. The day was,

likewise, a strategic choice because slaves from outlying plantations were frequently allowed to come to the city on Sundays.

Arms had been secretly manufactured by the slaves, but they
amounted to little more than crude pikes fashioned out of
sharpened poles. Vesey's real plans for combat included stealing
their masters' weapons, the transporting of hatchets and axes by
slaves from the countryside, and the seizing of the arsenal and
powderhouses throughout the city.

Once again, the well-laid plot was undone by a slave faithful
to his white master. The informant had become associated with
Vesey's rebels during their planning of the final operation. Once
the authorities investigated the plot, the leaders of the insurrection
were apprehended. Thirty-five, including Vesey, were hanged and
thirty-seven were deported from the United States. When the
authorities felt they had hanged enough to make an example, they
ceased the executions.

A third important anti-white uprising occurred in Southampton
County, Virginia, in 1831, and was led by a Negro mystic named
Nat Turner. Markings on Turner's head and breast were interpreted by other Negroes as signifying some special calling for him.
Turner read the Bible, led an extremely moral life, and claimed
to be in communication with spiritual voices which directed his
conduct.

A consciousness of his mission purportedly came to Turner
in 1825. Like ascetics of old, Turner labored daily to make himself
worthy. As he worked in the fields, he supposedly saw drops of
blood on the corn and white and black spirits contending in the
skies.

On May 12, 1828, Turner is said to have heard a great voice
saying that the Serpent was loosed, that Christ had laid down the
yoke, that he, Nat, was to take it up again, and that the time was
fast approaching when the first should be last and the last should
be first. An eclipse of the sun in February, 1831, was interpreted
by Turner as a sign to go forward.

Because he spent his time during the months preceding his
insurrection in prayer rather than in careful preparations and
recruitment, Turner was accompanied by only a small group of
slaves when he began his assault. The first target of Turner's band
was the household of Turner's master. After that slaughter, Turner's

band grew larger, though never reaching a total of more than 60 slaves at any time. Roaming throughout the countryside, they killed a total of 55 whites, including 10 men, 14 women, and 31 children.

The local militia and white vigilante groups began efforts to suppress the uprising immediately upon identifying the source of the violence. After six weeks of hiding, Turner and 46 other slaves were caught and tried: he and 16 of his followers were hanged.

While the three insurrections noted here were rather dramatic, it must be remembered that slave revolts were relatively common occurrences. Historian Herbert Aptheker has counted about 250 such uprisings.[4] Few of them were as dramatic as the three mentioned here, none of them was really successful or even of significant magnitude. As Frazier notes:

> During the nineteenth century many other slave plots and conspiracies were reported from various parts of the South ... There was considerable slave unrest resulting in sporadic conspiracies and attempted uprisings during the decade prior to the Civil War. These conspiracies and outbreaks involved slaves in Kentucky, Arkansas, Tennessee, Mississippi, Louisiana, and Texas.[5]

It must also be remembered that many small-scale revolts occurred but were never reported for fear that such reports would encourage other uprisings.

Several generalizations can be drawn from the historical data available on these and other slave insurrections. First, they were often led by inspired and/or intelligent or well-educated slaves. Second, they were expressions of extreme discontent with a system they sought to destroy. Historian Davidson Burns McKibben's commentary on these conclusions is of interest:

> The reasons for discontent culminating in revolt were many and varied. Professional agitators, abolitionists, white citizens raised in the South, combined with the slave population, and played an important part in fomenting radical, insurrectionary ideas. The French Revolution, success of the blacks on the island of Espanola in obtaining their freedom from the whites, and impossible promises by restless politi-

---

[4] Cited in Charles E. Silberman, *Crisis in Black and White* (New York: Random House, 1964), p. 79.

[5] Frazier, *op. cit.*, p. 89.

cians—all incited the Negroes, if not to direct action at least in thought.[6]

Although many strategies of insurrection were attempted, violence was involved in all of them. Despite their violent nature, they were singularly unsuccessful, either being discovered and quashed in the planning stages or being suppressed quickly after their outbreak. McKibben flatly asserts that "No organized revolt was ever successful."[7] Revolt scares, inspired by stories about actual uprisings or by rumors of plans for insurrection, were a common occurrence.

But, ultimately, these insurrections and revolts led only to the reassertion of the dominant pattern of the period: the suppressive violence on the part of the white master class simply increased in order to maintain domination over the slave.

LYNCHING

A second major pattern of violence in the United States is lynching. Common parlance has associated the term with hanging; however, technically, lynching includes a broader range of violent acts than hanging alone. In addition to hanging, the most common form of lynching, any group violence directed toward an individual or small group which results in the illegal death of the victim or victims should be considered as lynching.

The Tuskegee Institute, perhaps the nation's most complete source of data on this type of violence, has established four criteria which may be used to judge that an event constitutes lynching:

There must be legal evidence that a person was killed.
The person must have met death illegally.
A group must have participated in the killing.
The group must have acted under the pretext of service to justice, race, or tradition.[8]

That lynching has been an extremely common phenomenon in the United States is indicated in Table 6. Data prior to 1882, the

[6] Davidson Burns McKibben, "Negro Slave Insurrections in Mississippi, 1800–1865," *Journal of Negro History*, Vol. 34, 1949, pp. 89–90.

[7] *Ibid.*, p. 90.

[8] Tuskegee Institute, *1947 Negro Year Book* (Tuskegee, Alabama: The Negro Year Book Publishing Company, 1947), p. 303.

TABLE 6

LYNCHING BY DECADE
1882–1951

	Total Number Lynched	Average Annual Number Lynched	Number Negroes Lynched	Negroes as a Percentage of those Lynched %	Number Whites Lynched	Whites as a Percentage of those Lynched %
1882–1890	1299	144.3	619	47.7	680	52.3
1891–1900	1559	155.9	1132	72.6	427	27.4
1901–1910	846	84.6	752	88.9	94	11.1
1911–1920	606	60.6	554	91.4	52	8.6
1921–1930	275	27.5	248	90.2	27	9.8
1931–1940	114	11.4	103	90.4	11	9.6
1941–1951	31	2.8	29	93.5	2	6.5
TOTAL	4730	*	3437	72.7	1293	27.3

* This statistic would have little significance due to the overbalance of lynchings in the later 1880's and scarcity in the middle 1900's.

SOURCE: 1952 Negro Year Book, Tuskegee Institute, p. 278.

TABLE 7
LYNCHING BY REGION
1882–1946

	Number Whites Lynched	Whites Lynched as a Percentage of all Lynched in the Region	Number Negroes Lynched	Negroes Lynched as a Percentage of all Lynched in the Region	Total Number Lynched in the Region (Negro + White)	Percent Lynched in the Region as a Percentage of all Lynched in the U.S. (Negro + White)
North Eastern States	3	27.3	8	72.7	11	0.2
North Central States	270	63.7	154	36.3	424	9.0
Southern States	660	16.9	3245	83.1	3905	82.8
Western States	358	95.2	18	4.8	376	8.0
TOTAL	1291	27.4	3425	72.6	4716	100.0

SOURCE: 1947 Negro Year Book, Tuskegee Institute, p. 309.

year when the Tuskegee Institute began collecting lynching data, is extremely sketchy. There is, however, an indication that between 1871 and 1873, 75 lynchings occurred in the United States (25 per year). The Tuskegee Institute's data show that between 1882 and 1890, 1,299 lynchings, occurred (144.3 per year) ; and between 1891 and 1900, 1,559 lynchings occurred (155.9 per year). The largest single number of lynchings in one year (230) occurred in 1892.

From 1901 on, the number of lynchings began to decline. Between 1901 and 1910, the yearly average was 84.6 per year; between 1941 and 1950, it had dropped to a yearly average of only 2.8. Thus, lynching was most common from 1882 (when relatively accurate records begin) to the late 1910's, but then decreased rapidly as a major form of violence.

The critical observation, however, is that as lynching became less important as a general form of violence, it became steadily more of a racial phenomenon. The reason is relatively simple— as lynching became less socially acceptable as a method of 'taking the law into one's own hands against whites,' it became increasingly a method to 'keep niggers in their place.' Originally a means of seeking vengeance against anyone who had outraged or 'wronged' a community, it gradually became a phenomenon directed against Negroes as an act of social control—a warning to all persons of black skin that they occupied an inferior status.

Of the 1,299 lynchings between 1882 and 1890, only 47.7 per cent of the victims were Negroes. During the decade of the 1890's, 72.6 per cent of the 1,559 persons lynched were Negroes. Between 1910 and 1920, though the number of lynch victims dropped to 606, the percentage of the victims who were Negroes was 91.4. This figure stayed in the 90 per cent range after 1920, indicating that the decline in the use of lynching as a form of general social violence coincided with the increasing use of lynching as a pattern of violence against Negroes.

One further observation is pertinent. Table 7 indicates that the majority of lynchings from 1882 to 1946 (82.8 per cent of all lynchings) occurred in the South. And 83.1 per cent of all lynchings in the South were lynchings of Negroes.

These data reinforce the conclusion that lynching had become a predominantly racial phenomenon, but also indicate that lynching outside the South was less racially motivated than within the South. In the West, only 4.8 per cent of those lynched were Negroes. In the north central states, 36.3 per cent of all lynching victims were Negroes. Few lynchings were reported for the north east states.

Aggregating the statistics on lynching by year and by region, a trend becomes apparent. Over time, lynching became a significant phenomenon only in the South. And in the South, it was predominantly a racial phenomenon. As Myrdal summarizes:

> (Lynching) is one Southern pattern which has continued to arouse disgust and reaction in the North and has, therefore, been made much of by Negro publicists ... Since the early 1890's, the trend has been toward fewer and fewer lynchings ... The decrease has been faster outside the South, and the lynching of whites had dropped much more than that of Negroes. Lynching has become, therefore, more and more a Southern phenomenon and a racial one.[9]

There have been many *mob lynchings* in our nation's history. One which occurred in Omaha in 1919 [10] is summarized here as a model of this type of violence.

In late September of 1919, a young white Omaha girl named Agnes Labeck was raped. She thought her assailant was a Negro. The Omaha police subsequently forced forty 'undesirable' Negroes to leave town. On September 28 the police arrested a suspect. William Brown, a Negro, was incarcerated in the town jail, located on the first floor of the County Court House. That afternoon, crowds of whites began gathering outside the Court House. Expecting that trouble might occur, Sheriff Clark began massing police at the Court House.

Omaha's Mayor Smith refused to hand Brown over to the mob. But, while the mayor was making his appeal to the crowd to disband, the crowd grew unruly and attacked him. Placing a rope

[9] Gunnar Myrdal, *An American Dilemma* (New York: Harper & Row, 1944), pp. 560–561.

[10] For a detailed account of this incident, see: Arthur I. Waskow, *From Race Riot to Sit-In* (New York: Doubleday & Company, Inc., 1966), pp. 110–119; and the *New York Times, September 29–30, 1919*; for two brief accounts of this incident from Negro sources, see: "The Real Causes of Two Race Riots," *The Crisis*, Vol. 19, No. 2, pp. 61–62; and Tuskegee Institute, *Negro Year Book, 1921–1922* (Tuskegee, Alabama: Negro Year Book Company, 1922), p. 75.

around the mayor's neck, several Omaha citizens dragged him for half a block. The end of the rope was then thrown over a trolley pole. Twice the mayor's body was raised from the ground. Police officers arrived just in time to prevent the crowd from murdering their mayor. Though rumors later circulated that the mayor had indeed been killed, they proved false. The police took the severely injured mayor to a hospital.

As the sun set on Omaha, the mob sacked nearby gun supply stores, arming itself with weapons and explosives. Every street within a four-block radius of the Court House became jammed with people. At 7:00 P.M. the mob started a fire on the first floor of the Court House. When the Omaha Fire Department arrived to extinguish the blaze, the mob cut the firehoses. At 10:00 P.M. the mob threw fire bombs and cans of gasoline through the building's windows. The first four floors of the building soon were in flames. The police and prisoners had by this time moved upward to the fifth floor. Eventually, their retreat brought them to the building's roof.

The other prisoners, realizing that the building might collapse or that the crowd might not be satisfied with venting their anger only on Brown, urged the police to hand Brown over to the mob. In addition, some of the mob members had climbed to the roofs of adjoining buildings and began to fire at the group on the Court House roof.

After only fifteen minutes, the Sheriff and his assistants and prisoners were forced by gunfire back into the building. But some members of the crowd, finding an unburned passage, had entered the building by this time. They took Brown from the Sheriff and, according to some versions, had help from the other prisoners in the process. By now, the unburned passage had evidently been closed off, as ladders were leaned against the building. Brown, stripped naked, was brought down one of the ladders until he was about thirty feet from the ground. The mob members on the ladder then threw him off the ladder to the crowd below. They, in turn, rushed the injured Negro across the street and hanged him from an electric light pole. As he was hanging, his body was riddled with bullets. Later, it was removed and burned by the crowd.

Early in the evening, the police had asked for Army help from

Fort Crook and Fort Omaha. But the troops, delayed by red tape and lack of preparedness, did not begin marching soon enough. Only after a Nebraska senator called Secretary of War Newton D. Baker, who in turn called Fort Omaha directly, did the troops leave. Once they did arrive, the troops attempted, and with a good degree of success, to patrol the border between the white and Negro districts. Aerial reconnaisance, using an observation balloon, and strategically located machine guns aided in keeping the peace. Though still under heavy Army guard on September 30, the city began to return to normal.

The last year that the Tuskegee Institute reported on lynchings in the United States was 1952. Though for years its data had been used as an indicator of race relations in the nation, by 1952 they had become so infrequent that lynchings were no longer a meaningful index of racial harmony or hatred. No lynchings were reported anywhere in the country in 1952, and again in 1953. Thus, the *New York Times* reported:

> The Tuskegee Institute today announced its abandonment of its Annual Lynching Letter. "Lynching ... as a barometer for measuring the status of race relations in the United States, particularly in the South, seems no longer to be a valid index to such relationships."[11]

Just as slave rebellions had their heyday, so too lynchings for a time occupied a special prominence, both in overall and in racial violence in America. But by the early 1950's, lynching as a form of violence—racial or otherwise—was virtually non-existent.

WHITE-DOMINATED, PERSON-ORIENTED RIOTS

Distinct from lynching, white-dominated, person-oriented violence is not an attack upon specified individuals or specified groups of individuals. Rather, the attacks are directed upon whole communities of individuals. The attackers are white. The victims are Negroes. The violence originates with, and is directed and controlled by whites. Their aim is personal injury or death to Negroes. The Negroes, as victims, have historically done little to defend themselves. In the North, this form of violence has been termed rioting—that is, mobs of people collectively violating the

---

[11] *New York Times*, December 31, 1953.

law by attacking other groups. The model for this form of violence
is the race riot of 1908 in Springfield, Illinois.[12]

Prior to the August 14–15 riot, the city of Springfield had
been in a state of aroused tension for nearly four weeks over the
murder of a white man by a Negro. Joe James, a Negro tramp
addicted to drugs and alcohol, had been taken from a freight train
and jailed for thirty days as a vagrant. On the night of the murder
of Clergy A. Ballard, he had been released. According to the grand
jury indictment, James had entered the room of Ballard's daughter
at night, grappled with the irate Ballard, and fled. During the
struggle, Ballard was mortally injured. James was found asleep
in a park near the Ballard home the next day, under the influence
of drugs.

A similar incident actually touched off the rioting. On the night
of Friday, August 14, Mrs. Earl Hallam claimed to have been
attacked at her home by a Negro assailant. George Richardson
had been working on a neighboring lawn the day before the attack. The Negro gardener was accused by Mrs. Hallam and arrested the next day. (Richardson was exonerated after the rioting.
A special grand jury uncovered the fact that Mrs. Hallam had
been beaten by a white man, but not raped. She admitted that
Richardson had no connection with the affair and signed an
affidavit clearing him.)

On Saturday, August 15, rumors spread of the attack and of
Richardson's arrest. The community, already enraged over the
Ballard slaying, assembled outside the jail where both James and
Richardson were being held. The crowd demanded that both
prisoners be released to them for lynching. Sheriff Werner made
several efforts to maintain order, calling for more police officers
to guard the jail. But the mob continued to grow in numbers and
in anger. About 5:00 P.M. the crowd's attention was distracted
by a fire alarm. Sheriff Werner used the opportunity to slip James
and Richardson out of the jail and into the auto of a nearby
restaurant owner, Harry Loper. The prisoners were taken to the
Springfield railroad terminal, where the sheriff's deputies stopped

<hr>

[12] For a detailed account of this riot see: Chicago Commission on Race
Relations, *The Negro in Chicago* (Chicago: Unversity of Chicago Press,
1922), and the *New York Times*, August 16–18, 1908; Brawley, *op. cit.*,
p. 318.

a train, put the prisoners on board, and whisked them off to
Bloomington and, finally, the county jail at Peoria.

When the mob learned of this, it rushed to Loper's restaurant.
Loper appeared outside armed with a rifle, but the mob ignored
him and began throwing bricks through the restaurant windows.
When the mob had demolished the front of the restaurant, it
turned upon Loper's auto, smashing its windows and body. This
done, the mob set fire to both restaurant and auto.

The Springfield police were unable to control the rampaging
mob, as it cut firehoses to prevent the fire department from ex-
tinguishing the blazes. Nor were the police able to prevent the
mob from breaking into stores to secure guns, axes, and other
weapons.

Thus armed, the mob surged toward Springfield's Negro districts, systematically destroying homes and stores with fire bombs
and gasoline, and lynched several of the city's Negro residents.
One of the lynch victims was an 84-year-old Negro named Donegan. The mob hanged him from a tree. The rope slit his throat.
The mob was in the process of mutilating Donegan's nearly ex-
pired body, when police officers dispersed the crowd. Donegan
died one hour later. His particular offense: his wife was white.

The rioting, burning, and lynching continued into the night on
Friday and lasted through the entire following day. Before the
rioting ended, 5,000 militiamen (called for on Friday evening by
Illinois Governor Deneen) were patrolling the streets of Springfield. By Sunday, the situation was under control.

One of the distinctive factors about the riot was the reaction
of the Negro community to the white onslaught. For the most part,
they left their homes and fled in terror to safety. Many who remained were beaten severely or lynched. Only a few armed themselves and fought back. As the *Times* reported:

The situation of the Negroes is pitiful. In such places as have the
courage to retain them their fears show plainfully (sic) in grave fears
and their endeavors to keep out of sight of persons on the street ...
Adjt. General Scott to-night (i.e. Saturday night) estimated that fully
300 colored folk left the city since last night by train alone. Many
more, being without sufficient funds for the railroad trip, went to the
outskirts of the city by trolley and then, with their few belongings on
their backs, started to tramp across country in search of safety ...
Negroes innocent of any wrongdoing, or of any desire to harm the

whites, became panic stricken. With their houses burning, they loaded the trolley cars of the suburban lines, and made the stations of the railroads hulk with trembling black humanity. They were seeking places away from the city.[13]

The homeless Negroes swarmed into neighboring towns, including Chicago. Three thousand camped at Camp Lincoln, the National Guard training grounds. Within Springfield, about 2,000 Negroes gathered for protection inside the arsenal which was protected by both police and troops.

Even though the rioting was quieted by Sunday, Negroes continued to leave the city. Those leaving after the rioting were escorted to the train station by the troops. They were reported to be headed for places as far away as Missouri, Kentucky, and even into the Deep South.[14] On Monday the *Times* reported:

There are still many Negroes left in Springfield, but of these there are many who are planning to go at the first opportunity. In a week, it is predicted, the prosperous Negro colonies will be like deserted villages.[15]

The violence had been white-originated. It was also white-directed, and nearly totally white-dominated. It was largely person-oriented, although much property damage occurred along the way. Springfield's Negroes had not seriously attempted to resist the violence, nor did they seek to retaliate. They feared for their lives and, in large numbers, left the city.

In the South, a similar pattern developed. However, the white-dominated, person-oriented violence took a different form. Instead of rioting, Southern whites organized into 'night-riding' or vigilante groups. Organizations with a highly structured format, like the Ku Klux Klan, became common. Their purpose was systematic terrorization of the Negro community. A variety of techniques of physical punishment were employed, ranging from flogging to maiming, hanging, and murdering. All sorts of trivial and imagined offenses were revenged. Negroes were assumed to be 'bad' unless they proved otherwise by their submissive behavior.

Such terrorizing of the Negro community in the South began during Reconstruction. The precise number of Negroes killed during

---

[13] *New York Times*, August 16, 1908.
[14] *Ibid.*
[15] *New York Times*, August 17, 1908.

Reconstruction by vigilante violence will never be known. Sociologist Guy Johnson has indicated that five thousand Negro deaths during this period due to vigilante violence would be a "conservative estimate."[16] Johnson concluded that ". . . Reconstruction was in a sense a prolonged race riot."[17]

This type of violence continued steadily during the early 1900's. Although it began to taper off in intensity in the 1930's and 1940's, vestiges remain even today. Note, for example, the murder of three civil rights workers in Philadelphia, Mississippi in 1964. Less publicized than the brutal slayings of James Cheney, Andrew Goodman and Michael Schwerner was the fact that the search for these men uncovered four additional bodies in the Mississippi and Pearl rivers. How they died or who they were remains unknown, but there is reason to believe that their deaths were similar to those of Cheney, Goodman, and Schwerner.

The pattern of white-dominated, person-oriented violence in the relatively rural South consisted largely of marauding bands of whites attacking Negro communities and terrorizing the residents. But, where urban complexes sprang up in the South, the white-dominated, person-oriented violence followed the same pattern as that of the Springfield riot. The Atlanta race riot of 1906 is a perfect example.[18]

During the 1906 gubernatorial campaign in Georgia, one of the candidates—Hoke Smith—ran on a platform which included disenfranchising the Negro residents of the state. To win support for this measure, Smith's campaigners stirred up a good deal of anti-Negro sentiment throughout the state. At the same time, poor whites began to worry that Negro disenfranchisement would be followed by the disenfranchisement of poor whites. Both factors created tension between the races during the summer of 1906.

This tension was augmented by a rash of reported assaults of white women by Negroes. The *Atlanta News* exploited this situation by detailing, exaggerating, and even inventing stories about such incidents. (The Fulton County Grand Jury eventually brought

[16] Guy B. Johnson, "Patterns of Race Conflict," in Edgar T. Thompson (editor), *Race Relations and the Race Problem* (Durham, North Carolina: Duke University Press, 1939), p. 138.

[17] *Ibid.*

[18] For a detailed account of this riot see: E. Franklin Frazier, *op. cit.,* pp. 162–164; and Benjamin Brawley, *op. cit.,* pp. 318–320.

an indictment against the newspaper, charging that the *News* had been largely responsible for inciting the riot. As a consequence, Atlanta businessmen withdrew financial support from the *News*, forcing it to suspend publication.)

On Friday, September 21, a Negro was being tried for the rape of a white girl. The girl's father attempted to physically attack the Negro in open court. A small riot in the Court House was barely averted.

On Saturday, a throng of whites from Atlanta and neighboring towns became angered over stories in the evening *News*. The paper printed four extras that evening, each one carried through the streets by newsboys heralding the headlines. Each headline announced a new assault by a Negro upon a white woman. Under the influence of large quantities of liquor, the white mob assaulted Negroes whenever they appeared on the streets of Atlanta. The governor of the state mobilized the militia, but the crowd ignored the threat of troops. They received encouragement from Atlanta's mayor who announced that so long as Negroes committed crimes, they could expect to be dealt with in such a manner.

The aimless attacks by the white mobs against any and all readily available members of the black community continued until Tuesday. When a marauding band of whites led by a law officer entered the Negro district, the officer was shot and killed and some of his band wounded. Though only a few Negroes appeared to be engaging in self-defense of this sort, the shooting of the officer apparently gave sobering second thoughts to the white community. The militia was ordered into the Negro district. There, a search was conducted for weapons. Those arms which were uncovered were confiscated. Those persons suspected of having fired at the police or caught carrying concealed weapons were jailed. With this, the white community seemed reassured and their rioting ended.

The rioting was almost entirely one-sided. Myrdal notes that it was "more a one-way terrorization than a two-way riot."[19]

Other examples of this type of one-sided violence are notable throughout the late 1890's and early 1900's. They include riots in Wilmington, North Carolina (1896); Washington, D. C.

---

[19] Myrdal, *op. cit.*, p. 567.

(1919); East St. Louis, Illinois (1917); and Tulsa, Oklahoma (1921).

Perhaps the following description of the East St. Louis violence best synthesizes the elements of white-dominated, person-oriented violence:

> The July 2 killing of Negroes was indiscriminate ... Some of those who lost their lives were among the oldest and most respected colored people in the city. Most Negroes in the riot zone made no attempts to defend themselves, and the small number of casualties among the whites clearly showed the one-sidedness of the riot.[20]

RACIAL WARFARE, PERSON-ORIENTED RIOTING

The high degree of Negro passivity while under attack from marauding bands of whites did not remain as the dominant Negro response. Obviously, in a race riot, each race can engage in person-oriented violence against members of the other race. Such a situation may be termed racial warfare. The model chosen for this type of violence is the 1919 Chicago riot.[21]

Chicago's race relations were at a low ebb in 1919. For four years, young white toughs had been assaulting Negroes almost at will. The attacks reached a peak on June 21, 1919. That night, two Negroes were murdered by white hoodlums. Each of the victims had been alone at the time of his murder. And each was killed in an unprovoked though singularly brutal attack. In the four weeks prior to the rioting, twenty-four Negro homes were bombed. The police were unable to apprehend the guilty parties. Some persons charged that the police made no real effort to investigate the bombings. The general reason for the bombings was fairly apparent: whites were angered over Negroes moving into previously all-white neighborhoods.

On Sunday, July 27, at 4:00 P.M., 17-year-old Eugene Williams, a Negro, was swimming offshore at the Twenty-ninth Street Beach. The beach was used by both races. However, a tacit understanding had developed that part of the beach was reserved to whites and

---

[20] Elliot M. Rudwick, *Race Riot at East St. Louis* (Carbondale, Illinois: Southern Illinois University Press, 1964), p. 53.

[21] For a thorough discussion of the events in this riot, see: Chicago Commission on Race Relations, *op. cit.*, pp. 1–52; and Waskow, *op. cit.*, pp. 38–59; and *New York Times*, July 28–August 3, 1919.

part to Negroes. The imaginary dividing line even extended into the water.

Williams had entered the water at the Negro end of the beach, but swam in the direction of the white area and then drifted into it. Just before Williams was noticed crossing the imaginary dividing line, four Negroes had walked onto the white section of the beach. When white men ordered them away, they left. But they soon returned with other Negroes. This initiated a series of attacks and retreats by both whites and blacks. Both sides engaged in stone-throwing at each other; and the whites pelted the water around Williams as he floated with the aid of a railroad tie.

A white boy then swam toward Williams. Williams let go of the tie and, panicked, tried to swim away. After only a few strokes, Williams went under. (A coroner's jury later ruled that Williams had drowned because stone-throwing kept him from returning to shore. His body showed no bruises, however.) Rumors soon spread among the Negroes that Williams had drowned after being hit by the thrown rocks. Several Negroes claimed to have seen a particular white man throw the rock that struck Williams. The Negroes asked a white police officer to arrest the man, but the officer refused. Meanwhile, other Negroes—and whites—began to dive for Williams' body; simultaneously, the story of the officer's refusal to arrest the white man circulated through the crowd, angering the Negroes. The last straw for the Negroes occurred when the white officer, acting on the complaint of another white man, arrested a Negro. Nearby Negroes mobbed the officer. The riot was underway.

The Chicago Commission on Race Relations notes in its report on the riot that:

... first reports from the lake after the drowning indicated that the situation was calming down. White men had shown a not altogether hostile feeling for the Negroes by assisting in diving for the body of the boy. Furthermore, a clash started on the isolated spot could not be augmented by outsiders rushing in. There was every possibility that the clash, without the further stimulus of reports of the policeman's conduct, would have quieted down.[22]

As news of the events at the beach reached the nearby Negro ghetto, hundreds of Negroes began to converge on the beach area. Police reinforcements were summoned. While the law officers were

[22] Chicago Commission on Race Relations, *op. cit.*, p. 5.

assembling, a lone Negro fired upon them. A Negro policeman returned the fire and killed the gunman.

There were no further outbreaks on the beach. However, roving mobs and gangs engaged in sporadic clashes during the evening and early morning hours throughout the city. From 9:00 P.M. until 3:00 A.M., twenty-seven Negroes were beaten, seven were stabbed, and four were shot.

Few clashes occurred Monday morning as most people, of both races, went to work. But, as the afternoon wore on, white men and boys living between the stock yards and Chicago's Black Belt engaged in mob violence against Negroes returning home from work. Whites also thronged around streetcar tracks, pulling the trolleys from their wires so that Negro passengers could be dragged out and beaten.

By Monday night, organized gangs and bands were systematically terrorizing neighborhoods all over the city. Negroes, as well as whites, participated in the violence. Says the Chicago Commission:

The "Black Belt" contributed its share of violence to the record of Monday afternoon and Monday night. Rumors of white depredations and killings were current among the Negroes and led to acts of retaliation.[23]

Auto raids were added to Monday night's activities. Cars carrying white snipers moved at high speed through sections inhabited by Negroes. Negroes retaliated by sniping back, often from behind barricades or from ambush. So fearful were some Negroes of the motorized white snipers that they opened fire on all autos without waiting to see the intent or color of the occupants.

A general strike on the surface and elevated trolley lines began at midnight on Monday. As a result, clashes on and around the streetcars ceased. However, the trolley strike created new opportunities for violence to flare on Tuesday morning: men idled because of the lack of transportation congregated on the streets, thus increasing the gang warfare. Numerous other men, attempting to walk to work through hostile neighborhoods, were savagely attacked. Several were killed.

Later Tuesday morning, a white gang of soldiers, sailors, and

[23] *Ibid.*, p. 6.

civilians raided downtown Chicago, killed two Negroes, beat and robbed untold others, and wantonly destroyed the property of white businessmen.

Gang warfare continued into Tuesday night. Police officers were unable to control the rioting because of insufficient numbers. Though National Guard units had been assembled in Chicago as early as Monday evening, they were not put into the field until Wednesday, when the major violence had already come to an end.

The most important factor leading to the end of the rioting was the weather. Rain on Wednesday and Thursday drove members of both races into their homes. As the temperature fell, the violence became more sporadic, scattered, and minor.

Friday witnessed only a single reported injury. On Saturday morning 49 homes were burned in the immigrant neighborhood west of the stock yards. Nearly a thousand people, most Lithuanian immigrants, were made homeless as the fires did a quarter of a million dollars damage. Though responsibility for the fires was not (and never has been) fixed, the riot virtually halted on Saturday, with only a few injuries reported over the next several days.

Within a week, the riot zone had settled back to normal, and the militia was withdrawn. But, for seven days, there had been active warfare between whites and blacks in Chicago. And, for six additional days, feelings had been high enough to require the continued presence of the militia.

During those thirteen days, thousands were left homeless; 38 persons were killed (23 Negroes and 15 whites); and 537 were injured (342 Negroes, 178 whites, 17 undetermined). Amazingly, no hangings were reported.[24] In addition to these results, however, authorities in Chicago concluded that many injuries probably went unreported during the chaos, probably out of fear of arrest for participation.

The same pattern or racial warfare was repeated in the 1943 Detroit riot.[25] Though the exact events that started the riot are in

---

[24] *Ibid.,* p. 1.
[25] For a detailed account of this riot see: Alfred M. Lee and Normal D. Humphrey, *Race Riot* (New York: The Dryden Press, Inc., 1943); Robert Shogan and Tom Craig, *The Detroit Race Riot* (Philadelphia: Chilton Books, 1964); and the *New York Times,* June 21–23, 1943.

dispute, it is known that a fight began at the Belle Isle Park, Sunday evening (June 20, 1943). One version says that a white man and a Negro simply began fighting with each other. Other versions include the attack of two white girls by sailors, and the subsequent involvement of Negroes; the attack of two swimming white girls by Negroes; the throwing of a Negro baby from a bridge by whites; and the throwing of a white baby from a bridge by Negroes.

In any event, when the police arrived at the Belle Isle Bridge, 200 sailors were fighting with Negroes, and white civilians were joining the foray on the sailors' behalf. In 90 minutes, the fight on the bridge spread north and west, particularly into the Negro ghetto. Rumors and distortions preceded the violence as it grew and spread. By 1:00 A.M. the next morning (Monday), Negro rioters were roaming beyond Belle Isle. Injury cases were being received at Detroit's Municipal Hospital at the rate of one per minute.

The rioting continued throughout the night. By 3:00 A.M., Negroes had started looting stores owned by whites in the Paradise Valley area; an hour later whites had begun to attack Negroes as they emerged from the all-night movie theaters in downtown Detroit.

As the rioting continued into Monday (June 21), Mayor Jeffries and Governor Kelley considered and discarded several plans of action to quell the disturbances. Neither one wanted to suspend civil control and declare martial law. Instead, the governor banned the sale of alcoholic beverages, closed all amusement places at 9:00 P.M., and imposed an optional curfew from 10:00 P.M. to 6:00 A.M. by asking people "not having important business or going or coming from work" to stay in their homes.

The violence continued. In fact, it reached its peak of intensity Monday evening. White mobs attempted to invade the Negro slums of Paradise Valley. A group of police officers and Negro snipers fought a pitched battle at the Frazer Hotel on the ghetto's fringe; other police officers were shooting Negro looters. Mobs and gangs continued sporadic attacks, overturning parked autos and beating their occupants and pulling passengers off trolley cars for the same purpose. Attempted forays into the Negro slums by armed whites in autos were thwarted as snipers and groups of residents defending their property fired back.

Finally the governor took the steps necessary to call in Federal troops. By midnight on June 21, the U. S. Army had established an armed truce between Detroit's two warring factions. The presence of the troops maintained almost complete order on Tuesday and thereafter.

In less than three full days of rioting, 710 persons were killed or injured. Deaths totaled 34 (25 Negro, 9 white); injuries totaled 676 (254 Negro, 345 white, 77 police officers of both races); and property damage approximated two million dollars.[26]

The Chicago and Detroit riots were significantly different from earlier ones in that attacks originated on both sides and were both aimed at the persons of the opposing groups. Neither group accepted the attacks without retaliation. The result was racial warfare.

NEGRO-DOMINATED, PROPERTY-ORIENTED RIOTING

The final pattern of racial violence in our analysis is the Negro-dominated, property-oriented riot. Riots of this type are distinguished by the fact that Negroes initiate the violence and direct their hostilities towards property rather than towards persons. Most of the property is owned by whites, but located within the Negro ghetto. The violence hardly ever spreads outside the Negro neighborhoods to white residential areas or to such neutral areas as downtown locations.

The first major appearance of this type of violence occurred in Harlem in 1935.[27] On March 19, a seemingly unimportant incident occurred; a Negro youth stole a knife from a dimestore in the midst of Harlem. He was apprehended by the store's personnel and taken to the back of the store for questioning. When the child became hysterical, the store personnel released him into the store's

[26] Grimshaw, *A Study in Social Violence,* pp. 361–373.

[27] For a detailed account of this riot see: Harold Orlansky, *The Harlem Riot: A Study in Mass Frustration* (New York: Social Analysis, 1943); and Joseph Boskin and Frances Lomas Feldman, "Riots in the City," an addendum to the McCone Commission Report.

back alley. The crowd of shoppers inside the store was unaware of the true circumstances and surmised that the boy had been beaten by the white store personnel. The presence of a hearse in the alley added substance to the untrue rumor that the boy had been murdered—a rumor which quickly spread.

Within the hour, Negro and white pickets of the Young Liberators League gathered outside the store with signs reading: "Kress Brutally Beats Negro Child." One of the pickets was arrested for inciting to riot. The crowd which assembled to watch the proceedings pelted the police with rocks and bottles. Less than three hours later, over 3,000 Negroes were roaming the streets of Harlem, breaking store windows. Looting began after dark, with the most sought-after item being food (The Depression made conditions in Harlem even worse than usual in terms of availability of food). Incidents between Negroes and whites were minimal—with the exception of confrontations between the police and the looters. The looting of stores continued through Wednesday, March 20, but was finally brought under control through the efforts of police and local Negro leaders.

This pattern of Negro-dominated, property-oriented rioting was repeated in Harlem in 1943 and eventually become the model for much of the violence of the 1960's.

THE VIOLENCE OF THE 1960'S

Between 1935 and 1960, there were numerous violent racial incidents. The most dramatic was the 1943 Detroit riot previously discussed. However, it was not until the 1960's that rioting became a problem of national crisis proportions, and the pattern of Negro-dominated, property-oriented rioting became firmly established—at least for the present.

In 1964 there were major outbursts in Harlem, Rochester, Jersey City, Paterson-Elizabeth, Chicago, and Philadelphia; minor outbursts were numerous and widespread.

For the summers following 1964, it becomes nearly meaningless to simply list the racial outbreaks. The enumeration of cities adds little to our understanding of the events.

The Senate Permanent Investigating Committee, chaired by

Senator McClellan, has compiled a listing of *major* riots and civil-criminal disorders.[28] For 1965, *five* such incidents were listed, the most prominent of which is the Watts riot of August 11–18. The committee counted twenty major riots in 1966 of which the July 18–24 riots in Cleveland's Hough area and the September 28–October 2 riots in San Francisco are the most significant. For 1967, seventy-six major incidents are listed, dominated by Newark (July 12–16) and Detroit (July 23–31). This is not to imply that the other 1967 disorders are insignificant. All of the seventy-six outbreaks occurred between April 1 and September 8; a period of only five months.

July was by far the worst month, with 56 outbreaks occurring between July 1 and July 31, 1967. July 23 alone marked the beginning of riots in the following cities: Birmingham, Alabama; Detroit, Michigan; Lima, Ohio; New Britain, Connecticut; New York City, New York; Phoenix, Arizona; Rochester, New York; Toledo, Ohio; Tucson, Arizona; and Kalamazoo, Michigan. By the end of the summer in 1967, twenty-eight states plus the District of Columbia had experienced civil violence.

Any number of incidents could be used as a model of the violence of the 1960's. Newark was chosen because the riot there demonstrates the Negro-dominated, property-oriented riot pattern operating at a full scale. Not all riots in the 1960's demonstrate everything that occurred there; some never developed as fully. However, an analysis of Newark does suggest what occurs when a riot develops fully into the Negro-dominated, property-oriented pattern.

NEWARK, NEW JERSEY

There are various versions about the precise way the riot started; however, all versions involve a confrontation between two police officers, John DeSimone and Vito Pontrelli, and a Negro cab driver, John Smith. The Governor's Select Commission on Civil Disorder which Governor Richard Hughes of New Jersey established to examine the Newark riot heard conflicting testimony

[28] "Major Riots, Civil-Criminal Disorders," prepared for Permanent Subcommittee on Investigations of the Government Operations Committee, U. S. Senate.

on the incident.[29] The police officers testified that they were on a routine patrol at dusk on July 12, when a taxi cab pulled up close behind them, alternatively began breaking and accelerating, with its high beam flickering on and off. In this manner, the patrolmen testified that the cab tailgated their patrol car for almost a block. The cab then shot around them, passing them and proceeding on while travelling in the wrong lane. The patrolmen pursued the cab and stopped it.

DeSimone and Pontrelli's version claims that they then asked Smith to show his license. He refused, answering with insults and curses. When told he was going to be arrested, Smith opened the door of his cab, striking DeSimone in the chest and punching him in the face. The two officers then subdued Smith, called another patrol car to tow the cab, and started for the police station. When at the station, Smith refused to leave the car or to walk. The police were forced to pull him from the car and drag him into the station.

Smith's version of the encounter is drastically different. He claims that he picked up a woman passenger near the City Hospital on the evening of July 12. He encountered the police car which was double parked. Smith claims he gave a signal and legally passed the parked police car. The police, however, immediately pursued and stopped him.

In the encounter that followed, Smith claims he was rudely arrested while his passenger was insulted and asked to leave the cab. On the way to the police station, Smith was supposedly severely beaten by one of the policemen. Because of a painful blow in the groin, Smith was unable to walk from the car to the police station. Once in the station, the physical brutality inflicted upon him by the police was intensified.

This might have been the end of the whole incident: however, Smith was seen being taken into the police station by the Negro residents of the Hayes Homes housing development. They observed

[29] Governor's Select Commission on Civil Disorders, *Report for Action*, State of New Jersey, February, 1968, pp. 104–106. In addition to the above, for a detailed account of this riot see: Tom Hayden, *Rebellion in Newark: Official Violence and Ghetto Response* (New York: Random House, 1967); *Report of the National Advisory Commission on Civil Disorders*, (Washington, D. C.: Government Printing Office, March, 1968); and the *New York Times*, July 13–17, 1967.

what they presumed to be a battered Negro. At the same time, reports circulated over the VHF cab radio band that white police had killed a Negro cab driver.

Within minutes, cabs and crowds converged on the police station. By midnight, rocks, bottles, and molotov cocktails were being hurled into the station. Less than half an hour later, looting began in the Negro district. A show of police force was made, and by 5:00 A.M. all was silent. There was still some uncertainty as to whether the rioting had ceased or would resume again on the next day.

On Thursday, Newark's Mayor Addonizio called in civil rights leaders, including several moderate ministers and some of the more militant individuals. Tom Hayden describes the meeting in his account of the violence of Newark:

> Concessions were made. Addonizio decided to ask for City Council funds to allow additional police captaincies so that a qualified Negro officer, Eddie Williams, could become the first Negro captain. He requested that Human Rights Director James Threatt and Police Director Dominick Spina separately investigate Wednesday's conflict. He reassigned the two policemen who beat Smith to "administrative positions." He referred the Smith case to the county prosecutor and FBI. He announced formation of a Blue Ribbon Commission, like the McCone Commission that investigated Watts, to examine this "isolated incident."[30]

However, this did not satisfy the Negro community. A meeting was organized for that evening. Negroes gathered outside the police station to protest the unsatisfactory state of affairs. The demonstration began nonviolently as planned. However, after a few confrontations with the police, the demonstrations became violent. The violence at the police station spread to the Negro district, where looting and burning began. Police were called out in force; however, they were unable—despite many arrests—to bring the situation under control. The violence which had started at the police station in the Negro neighborhood had, by Thursday evening, spread uncontrollably.

At 2:30 A.M. on Friday, July 14, Mayor Addonizio called the Governor of New Jersey, Richard J. Hughes. The governor traveled to Newark immediately. He and the mayor began to patrol through

---

[30] Hayden, *op. cit.*, pp. 23–24.

the riot area, starting at 5:00 A.M. Returning from this inspection, the governor called the damage "unbelieveable." A state of emergency was declared and the National Guard was called into Newark.

Throughout the day of the 14th, 3,000 National Guard troops and about 375 state police patroled the Negro area where the rioting had occurred. But the burning and looting continued even with the troops present. On the afternoon of the 15th (Saturday), the first full day after the troops arrived, several hundred Negro volunteers wearing chartreuse armbands moved through the Negro ghetto and urged the residents to 'play it cool.' Even this, however, was insufficient to stop the riot activity which continued throughout Saturday.

It was not until July 17 (Monday) that Hughes declared that the state of emergency had ended and ordered the troops out of Newark. However, by that time, the damage had been done. One law officer, one fireman, and 23 Negro civilians had been killed, 145 law officers and 580 civilians had been injured. A total of 1,465 persons were arrested: 1,394 Negroes; 50 whites; and 21 Puerto Ricans. Insured property losses were estimated at over $15 million. Uninsured losses were indeterminate.

The Negro community had led the rioting; the hostility was mainly aimed at property; the only persons injured by Negroes were policemen.

ANALYZING THE PATTERNS

The patterns we have identified have occurred in historical sequence: *suppression and insurrection; lynching; white-dominated, person-oriented rioting; racial warfare, person-oriented rioting;* and *Negro-dominated, property-oriented rioting.* However, there is a considerable overlap between the patterns. When the first major Negro-dominated, property-oriented rioting occurred in Harlem, for instance, this did not mean that the racial warfare, person-oriented pattern would never again occur. In fact, it did in Detroit in 1943. What we have indicated is that each pattern was, *for a time,* barely noticeable, then gradually more important, and finally the dominant pattern of racial violence was gradually to be replaced by the emergence of another dominant pattern.

An analysis of the patterns gives rise to a partially empirical, partially theoretical cycle: at first, the white element was the dominant factor in the violence; gradually Negroes began to assert themselves by equal participation in the violence; then the Negroes began to assert themselves as the dominant factor in the violence. The dominance in violence of the Negro is not yet complete, assuming the patterns operate in a full cycle. The Negro-dominated rioting is still oriented toward white property and not the white person. If the patterns operate in a full cycle, the Negro would next orient his violence toward the white person, not the white's property—just as the whites initially oriented their violence towards the persons of their slaves. In any event, the Negro is dominant in this final pattern; in fact, virtually the only white participation is that of white police or other organized forces that attempt to suppress the riot.

This empirical-theoretical cycle of violence is congruent with the theme developed earlier, concerning the pattern of Negro-white relations in American society. We suggested that, as a slave, the Negro was entirely subservient to the white society. This relationship continued, albeit in a different though equally intense manner, with the Jim Crow system of the South and with the segregated ghettoized system of urbanization. Only with wartime demands did new opportunities for progress open to Negroes. As they opened, and the Negro achieved some gains, he participated in open warfare with whites. As America approached the 1954 recognition of *de jure* equality, the position of the Negro began to improve—slightly. The Negro began to assert himself, and the white man was forced to at least recognize that the assertion was occurring. With the subsequent Negro drive for *de facto* equality, the Negro further asserted himself. Although the Negro has not yet achieved equality, he nonetheless is aggressively pressing for it in the current pattern of interracial relations. It is the Negro who is making the demands and choosing the tactics; the white community basically has assumed the role of making a response to the Negro's lead. In Chapter Two, we described the increasingly intensified demands of the Negro after he had achieved *de jure* recognition. In Chapter Four, we discussed the *de facto* inequality which is still the predominant condition of the Negro in America. Here we contend that the assertive position of the Negro, after the white recognition of his *de jure* rights, has placed him in the leadership role of determining the future patterns of inter-racial relations. The Negro challenges; the white community responds.

This is not to say that the white community's response is un-important. Indeed, it is probable that the white community's an-swer to the Negro's demands will, in fact, determine the eventual outcome of the patterns of interracial relations. But, it cannot be denied that the Negro is now 'calling the shots.' When whites con-trolled the pattern of race relations, they took the lead in violence. As whites and Negroes approached an equality of dominance, both participated in violence. Now, as Negroes increasingly determine the affairs between the two races, they also behave more violently.

Political scientists have often defined the authority of a political system in terms of the system's legitimate monopoly over the mechanisms of violence. Thus, in the final analysis, the system maintains order by the use or threat of force. Perhaps, in race relations, a similar phenomenon has occurred. As one or the other race dominated the racial pattern, it simultaneously dominated violence.

Table 8 shows the patterns of violence in chronological order. The first four patterns have already occurred. The last three pat-terns would appear to be some of the possible future alternatives, assuming that violence continues between races and swings full-cycle back to person-oriented rioting with one race or the other dominating, or both races participating, in the spectrum of vio-lence.

In this context, two of the patterns would appear to be anom-alies: the slave revolts and the property-oriented rioting.

Turning first to the slave revolts, it is possible to hypothesize that they were simply expressions of extreme opposition to the entire slave system. If so, the revolts were an attempt to alter the status of racial relations, an attempt by the Negroes involved to move out of a subordinate position in race relations. In this light, the revolts may have been merely an early expression of a later trend. However, the white monopoly over the mechanisms of vio-lence doomed the revolts to total failure. Whites, through violence, were able to maintain their dominant position in the master-slave relationship.

TABLE 8

PATTERNS OF VIOLENCE

I	*Slavery*	White-dominated	Person-oriented
	Insurrections	Negro-dominated	Person-oriented
	Suppression	White-dominated	Person-oriented
II	*Lynching*	White-dominated	Person-oriented
	Rioting	White-dominated	Person-oriented
III	*Warfare*	White/Black-dominated	Person-oriented
IV	*Rioting*	Negro-dominated	Property-oriented
V	*Rioting* or	Negro-dominated	Person-oriented
	Warfare or	White/Black-dominated	Person-oriented
	Suppression	White-dominated	Person-oriented

In the Negro-dominated, property-oriented rioting of the 1960's, it is possible to see a similar phenomenon. Negroes rioting against the property of whites demonstrated their new-found position of leadership in the racial pattern. White-owned property in the ghetto is a symbol of "the man," the black man's term for the whole figure of oppression. Thus, the Negro can attack wantonly the property of the white man in the ghetto and derive satisfaction from the attack on the symbol.

However, were the Negro to engage in similarly massive violence against the white person outside the ghetto, the maximum suppressive force controlled by whites might well be brought to bear. The resulting possibility of severe repression of blacks under such circumstances cannot be ignored. The symbolic attack upon white property is a significant new dimension in racial violence both because it demonstrates intensified black self-exertion and because it subtly underscores the reality of a white controlled society, including a white controlled police force.

This analysis, however, does not mean that Negro-dominated violence must restrict itself to attacks upon white-owned property within the ghetto. It is well within the realm of possibility that black militants may begin to consider and plan attacks upon high-value white-owned property, perhaps even including such vital installations as power plants, transportation centers, reservoirs, etc.

It is also conceivable that greater emphasis may be placed upon inflicting harm upon white individuals. Perhaps, at first, such attacks may lie on a symbolic level as was the case with the initiation of attacks on white-owned property. Here, attacks upon policemen, firemen, and national guardsmen drawn into a riot situation gain significance. Sniping can take on a more meaningful role in such confrontations. It is even possible that black militants may begin to consider such attacks on white individuals drawn into a riot context as the primary objective of the violence underway.

An objective analysis of the nature of racial violence in American history underscores the change from white dominance to Negro dominance. The corresponding change in the overriding pattern of interracial relations is more difficult to document. Black men have internalized the nature of their 'place' in the society at various periods of time. Their articulation of how they view their role in American society is extremely illuminating. The significant change from the statements of leaders like Booker T. Washington to those of leaders like Martin Luther King, Jr., or Stokely Carmichael presents evidence of the changing 'place' of the black man in American society that is every bit as compelling as the evidence of the black man's role in violence has been. The Negro wants full participation in American society—now! He no longer says, as did Booker T. Washington, that the Negro should move slowly and prove his worth to the white man, before he 'requests' improvement in his situation.

Washington's approach was never universally accepted. But he did express an attitude that many whites and some Negroes held —an attitude the white man wished the Negro to internalize. Washington believed he was verbalizing the 'spirit of the time.' Perhaps the best statement of this spirit came in his 1895 address to the Atlanta Exposition. This speech established Washington in a nearly undisputed position of spokesman for the Negro in America, at least in the minds of whites:

The wisest among my race understand that the agitation of questions of social equality is the extremest folly, and that progress in the enjoyment of all the privileges that will come to us must be the result of severe and constant struggle rather than of artificial forcing.[31]

Washington's position was clear: The Negro must be patient; he must first improve himself and prove his worth to the white community; the gains and benefits would come.

Washington's position is even more clearly expressed in his book *The Future of the American Negro*. Once again, he argues the Negro's dependence upon the white man:

We must admit the stern fact that at present the Negro, through no choice of his own, is living among another race which is far ahead of him in education, property, experience, and favorable condition; further, that the Negro's present condition makes him dependent upon the white people for most of the things necessary to sustain life, as well as for his common school education. In all history, those who have possessed the property and intelligence have exercised the greatest control in government, regardless of colour, race, or geographical location.[32]

Washington began from the premise that Negroes were dependent upon whites. He opposed any violent means to achieve progress. He even opposed Negroes moving North to escape. He rather felt that the Negro should stay in the South's agricultural economy, develop skills there, and then move into other occupations. Gradually the Negro would prove his worth to the white man and be accepted as a valuable and needed part of the society. The Negro must improve himself to prove his worth:

I do not believe that the world ever takes a race seriously, in its desire to enter into the control of the government of a nation in any large degree, until a large number of individuals, members of that race, have demonstrated, beyond question, their ability to control and develop individual business enterprises. When a number of Negroes rise to the point where they own and operate the most successful farms, are among the largest taxpayers in their country, are moral and intelligent, I do not believe that in many portions of the South such men need long be denied the right of saying by their votes how

[31] Booker T. Washington, "Platform of Accommodation," in Francis L. Broderick and August Meier (editors), *Negro Protest Thought in the Twentieth Century* (New York: The Bobbs-Merrill Company, Inc., 1965), p. 7.
[32] Booker T. Washington, "The Future of the American Negro," in Broderick and Meier, *op. cit.*, p. 13.

they prefer their property to be taxed and in choosing those who are to make and administer the laws.[33]

Although opposition was expressed to this theory, its 'don't rock the boat' theme still pervades the thinking of many Negroes. But overwhelming evidence indicates that this is changing very rapidly.

The objective facts we have discussed—the segregation and the resultant underprivileged conditions which go with it—have nonetheless all resulted from something more pervasive than the Negro's acceptance of slow progress: namely, the white desire and actions to keep the Negro in his 'place.' This has been the real impact of Jim Crow, and the real cause of the ghetto. The white man has regarded the Negro as inferior and the Negro has internalized this belief.

In his book *Black Bourgeoisie* E. Franklin Frazier tells the story of the Negro youth who was asked if he felt inferior in the presence of white people. He gave the following answer.

Off-hand, I'd say no, but actually knowing all these things that are thrown up to you about white people being superior—that they look more or less down upon all Negroes—that we have to look to them for everything we get—that they'd rather think of us as mice than men—I don't believe I or any other Negro can help but feel inferior. My father says that it isn't so—that we feel only inferior to those whom we feel are superior. But I don't believe we can feel otherwise. Around white people until I know them a while I feel definitely out of place. Once I played a ping-pong match with a white boy whose play I know wasn't as good as mine, and boys he managed to beat I beat with ease, but I just couldn't get it out of my mind that I was playing with a white boy. Sort of an Indian sign on me, you know.[34]

Perhaps Booker T. Washington was right in realizing that the white segment of American society was in control and the Negro dependent upon that control. However, he was optimistic in believing the Negro could surmount that and prove his excellence. What happened in most cases was that the Negro developed an internal image of himself as truly inferior.

The continuing struggle to gain the rights granted in 1954 and afterward caused both white and black America to question that

[33] *Ibid.*, pp. 16–17.
[34] E. Franklin Frazier, *Black Bourgeoisie* (New York: Collier Books, 1957), p. 177.

role of inferiority. The civil rights movement gave the Negro a vehicle for demanding a rightful and equal place in society. The Negro began to assert himself. Martin Luther King, Jr. recognized and cultivated the Negro's new role. When King surveyed the civil rights movement in 1957, he noted:

For hundreds of years Negroes had fought to stay alive by developing an endurance to hardship and heartbreak. In this decade the Negro stepped into a new role. He no longer would endure; he would resist and win. He still had the age-old capacity to live in hunger and want, but now he banished these as his lifelong companions. He could tolerate humiliation and scorn, but now he armed himself with dignity and resistance and his adversary tasted the gall of defeat.[35]

The Negro no longer accepts a second-class role for himself; rather:

By 1967 the resounding shout of the Negro's protest had shattered the myth of his contentment. The courage with which he confronted enraged mobs dissolved the stereotype of the grinning, submissive Uncle Tom. Indeed, by the end of a turbulent decade there was a new quality to Negro life. The Negro was no longer a subject of change; he was the active organ of change. He powered the drive. He set the pace.[36]

The days of accommodation are over. The inferiority complex was considered, questioned and discarded. The Negro now demands to be heard. White America will respond. Or will it? And, if so, how? A 21-year-old Harlem resident told Dr. Kenneth Clark in 1965:

... I had a cop walk up to me a couple of days ago. You know what he said? "Move over." They have the street blocked up and he's going to tell me you can go around them. I said, "Hell if I do." He said, "What did you say?" I said, "Hell if I do." He said, "I'll slap your black ass." I told him, "That's one day you'll know if you're living or dying." He just looked at me ...[37]

[35] Martin Luther King, *Where Do We Go From Here?* (New York: Harper & Row, 1967), p. 16.
[36] *Ibid.*, p. 18.
[37] Kenneth B. Clark, *Dark Ghetto* (New York: Harper & Row, 1965), p. 5.

chapter six

THE NEW AMERICAN DILEMMA

INTRODUCTION

The police officer just looked. And all over America, other police officers, and other whites, looked. Some tried to find reason for the violence and destruction around them and tried to understand. Some cajoled and criticized or simply found support for their long-established hatreds. But they all looked. And most recognized that something was wrong, but hoped that the violence would somehow end.

But white America was not alone in its quandary. Most of black America also looked. Some asked if it was worth it all and tried to quiet a rampaging people. Others cried for more of the same and sowed seeds they hoped would grow into new types of violence. But they all looked. And most recognized the simultaneous excitement and horror that accompany violence, and wondered if it would end.

Black America has violently asserted itself throughout the last five summers, but the future course of black America is uncertain. Many captains are seeking the allegiance of a crew, still unsure that any of the ships will be able to chart a course to freedom. White America is responding, sometimes with violence, sometimes with only angry words, and even sometimes in a way that bodes hope for peace and progress. Whatever its other reactions, white America is shocked and more than just a little afraid.

Thus far, we have developed four major themes:

The Negro has won *de jure* recognition and is pressing for *de facto* equality (Chapter two).

As the pressure for improved (in fact, equal) objective conditions continues, a dispute over the method to be used in achieving equality has arisen. The radical approaches of black nationalism and black power are getting serious consideration (Chapter three).

The *de facto* condition of the Negro has been one of nearly total segregation into miserable conditions. Even the vigorous civil rights movement since 1954 (based largely upon a predominant attachment to nonviolence) has done little to change these conditions (Chapter four).

The objective pattern of interracial violence in the United States demonstrates that the Negro engaged in violence is closely paralleling his general move for *de jure* and then *de facto* equalization (Chapter five).

Our purpose in this chapter is to show more clearly the interrelationship of these themes and the ramifications of that interrelationship. Before we examine this, it is absolutely essential to realize something about ourselves as a people.

That many Americans, black and white, are disturbed by the wave of racial violence which has engulfed the nation since 1964 is not surprising. We have already noted a peculiar characteristic of our society which makes us grossly short-sighted about both the past and the future. Only the present is of real concern. Perhaps it is the relative youth of the American nation and its culture which prevents us from taking the long view. Perhaps only centuries more of growth and development will give this nation the finely honed "sense of the historical" often claimed by our European counterparts. Perhaps there is merit in living only from day to day. For it may be that a realization that there are, for example, recognizable patterns of racial violence will in no way help us avoid the violence which has not as yet emerged. Such a realization might paralyze our nation, or make it paranoid. But it is possible that we have already accomplished one or both.

The answers to these questions lie outside the scope of this work. The theoretical framework which follows is an attempt to place the violence of the 60's in perspective; to identify the long-standing anomaly within the very structure of our society which makes violence an integral part of our society and yet, at the same time, completely unfathomable and shocking to most of us. Undoubtedly, we will raise many issues and questions for which no adequate explanations or answers are available. For this we make no apology.

THE GREAT EXPERIMENT

Lyndon Johnson was in no way original in his emphasis on "consensus politics." Long before the inception of the United States as a sovereign entity, philosophers toyed with the notion that men could live together in a more or less harmonious relationship if agreement could be reached on certain basic assumptions about the nature of the social order.

Rousseau, Condorcet, Hobbes, Spinoza, Hume, and Locke were in basic agreement that some form of relationship among men allows for human coexistence on a plane more civilized than that of a savage. Their disagreements occurred in their perception of the nature of this relationship and the implications of that nature for the forms of socio-political organization which would or should result.

Which of these philosophers' particular orientations served as a model for the Founding Fathers is a moot question. The fact remains that, theoretically, the social and political structure of America rests on the assumption of a reasonable degree of consensus on basic values and the methods of achieving them. Not satisfied with previous formulations of this consensus, the Founding Fathers sought to implement the idealistic notion of a nation based on a representative form of participatory democracy.

Implicit in this assumption (at least it is implicit if the Founding Fathers' *idealistic* notion is to be successful) was a society of competing groups, none of which was strong enough to continually dominate the others. Agreement could be reached among these groups for several reasons:

> having certain interests in common, there was a common meeting point from which to begin negotiations;
> often having common, overlapping memberships, a premium was placed on compromise; and

their common heritage and cultural orientations narrowed the range of disagreement to areas which were not 'life and death' matters for the losing group.

Essentially, then, the success of the system depended upon a pluralistic society (in which cleavages were cross-cutting) in which none of the areas of contention among competing groups were so crucial to one group that losing out would critically and permanently impair that group's status.

In this situation, a coalition of groups sufficiently large could achieve its goals through the political system without risking anything more than the antagonism of the losers. The winning coalition's victory would not be a challenge to the legitimacy of the system which allowed the victory, because the losers would be willing to accept, for the moment (albeit on occasion with something less than grace), the outcome as a legitimate loss in the game of 'give-and-take.' Since the competing groups realign themselves relatively frequently, none are ever left entirely out for a long period of time. Everybody wins some and loses some of the contests over the authoritative allocation of values and resources. Theoretically, such a system minimizes the possibility of violence.

VIOLENCE IN AMERICA

Despite the grand design of the Great Experiment, however, violence is an integral part of the American way of life. Major social changes in this country, including the assimilation of many minority groups, have, almost without exception, been accompanied by violence.

A portent of things to come, our first major social crisis occurred when we expelled the British from our shores to gain independence. "This was accomplished by seven years of warfare, in which 25,000 in the Continental Army were killed, about one out of every eight men who served. To judge the extent of this violence one would have to consider that the same ratio of dead in our present population would amount to a death list of one and a half-million."[1]

[1] Howard Zinn, "Violence and Social Change in American History" (unpublished paper, presented at the University of Pennsylvania's Conference on Violence in Contemporary American Society, May 25–27, 1967), p. 2.

A series of violent acts, mostly directed at the American Indians, achieved our second great social accomplishment: conquest
of the entire continental land mass from East to West. The effec-
tiveness of our out-group hostilities is suggested by the decline of
the Indian population between Columbus' time and the present
(then, one million—now, about 400,000).[2] Further territorial ag-
grandizement came not only as the result of shrewd political and
diplomatic maneuvering (e.g., the acquisition of the Louisiana and
Oregon territories) but also as a result of violent military harass-
ments (to obtain East Florida) and a full-scale war (to obtain all
our Southwestern states from New Mexico to California).[3]

One of the most violent outbursts this nation has ever experienced achieved two outcomes of major social consequence: the
maintenance of the Federal Union and the abolition of slavery.[4]

Full-scale industrialization and the development of major urban
areas came only with violence of a different sort. "Those who
worked on the railroads, in the mines, in the factories and mills
were subjected to a kind of servitude destructive of both body and
spirit."[5] The major economic dislocations of the 1870's and the
1890's likewise caused violent hardships for millions of Americans.[6]

Even the nascent stages of welfarism, beginning in the Progres-
sive period, came only as a result of the hardships of earlier economic dislocations and the violence of early labor struggles: the
list of the latter reads like a Who's Who of violent episodes, including the railroad strikes of 1877, the Haymarket Riot of 1886,
the Homestead strike of 1892, the Pullman strike of 1894, the
Colorado Coal strike of 1913–1914.

The current movement for freedom and equality of the Negro
has been anything but nonviolent. Although members of the movement themselves had not engaged in violence (at least from 1955
through 1963), their tactics have in large measure depended upon

[2] *Ibid.*, p. 3.
[3] For an enlightening discussion of this period see the classic work
of Frederick Jackson Turner, "The Significance of the Frontier in American
History," *Annual Report*, American Historical Association (Washington,
1893).
[4] Zinn, *op. cit.*, p. 5.
[5] *Ibid.*, p. 6.
[6] *Ibid.*

the violent response of the white community to gain sufficient sympathy for their cause. What small gains the Negro has made, in the way of eliminating *de jure* segregation, could not have been achieved without violence.

Besides violence associated with major social changes in this nation, the United States has a long tradition of conflict and violence focussed on religion and ethnicity. Three religious groupings have been particularly singled out in our history for 'punishment' for their religious beliefs: Catholics, Jews, and Mormons.[7] Similarly, at one time or another, the Irish, Italians, Puerto Ricans, Mexican-Americans, etc., have been accorded violent treatment by their 'more American' neighbors. In like manner, the familiar traditions of violence in the Old West and the American underworld are indicative of strong undercurrents of violence running throughout our society.

Perhaps, however, the most clear-cut and continuous case of violence as part of the American way of life relates to Negro-white relations. Although, as we indicated in the last chapter, the patterns of this violence have changed at different historical periods, its almost continuous nature is a hard blow to the American dream.

Why, in a nation founded upon a philosophy of consensual decision-making, should violence be so prevalent—and prevalent at some of the most critical junctures in our history? The answer seems to lie in the consistent inability of a nation to match its political philosophy with the realities of its social composition.

At various times in our nation's history, one or another of the prerequisites for consensual harmony simply was absent. Either (a) common interests were lacking, (b) crosscutting cleavages were not in evidence, (c) issues became a matter of life or death, or (d) one group completely and invincibly dominated another.

If (a), (b), or (c) was the case, a minority group simply could not elicit enough support in the rest of the society to form a winning coalition. If condition (d) existed the dominant group could act without considering the consequences to the minority or minorities.

If a minority group was incapable of forming a winning coali-

[7] Allen Grimshaw, "Lawlessness and Violence in America," *Journal of Negro History*, Vol. 44, 1959.

tion, there were two alternatives for the minority: accept the un-desirable situation, or exercise the final option to produce a change, namely, engage in violence. As we shall see, violence often serves to create a bargaining situation for competing groups, generally with the majority making concessions to the minority for the preservation of peace.

Examples of the second alternative include the activities of the colonists during the Revolutionary War, much of the violence associated with industrialization, urbanization, and unionization, the violence-inducing nonviolence of Dr. King, and much of the violence visited upon religious and ethnic groups throughout our nation's history.

If the majority is invincible, the minority has no viable option: it must knuckle under to the demands of the majority until those demands are satisfied, engage in suicidal violence, or hope the majority relents.

Examples of these alternatives are less clear-cut, for several of the groups involved engaged in one or more of them at different historical junctures. The Indians for a time engaged in suicidal violence, but eventually capitulated to the white man. The Negro engaged in suicidal violence during his insurrectionary days, but was forced into submission during and following the Reconstruction era. And, if the Confederacy can be viewed as a large minority group, it first engaged in political violence but, when suppressed, accepted the Reconstruction occupation until such time as the majority (the North and its Congress) relented in the 1877 Compromise.

THE AMERICAN DILEMMA OF GUNNAR MYRDAL

In his classic study, *An American Dilemma*,[8] published in 1944, Gunnar Myrdal probed the inconsistency which underlies American interracial relations. The American people had traditionally accepted an equalitarian doctrine: that 'all men are equal' and that this equality is to extend to every individual regardless of race, creed, or color. At the same time, slavery had been an established

[8] Gunnar Myrdal, *An American Dilemma* (New York: Harper & Row, Publishers, 1944). See especially pp. 1–112.

pattern. Even after the abolition of slavery, the nation maintained a caste-like system wherein the white race ruled and the Negro was relegated to a separated and subordinated position.

This constituted a dilemma. If all were equal, the Negro must be equal also. However, the objective reality of the Negro's condition and the attitudes held toward him gave every indication that the Negro was not equal.

For most white Americans, this intellectual difficulty probably did not present a serious problem. The majority of white individuals in the country was basically ignorant of the Negro's situation. If aware of it, the white man did his best to forget it. The Negro, on the other hand, could not be ignorant of this situation: segregation and subjugation within the caste system was his way of life.

Myrdal observed that those individuals in the society who were aware of the contradiction and the inconsistency in the treatment of the Negro found a method of rationalization which enabled them to maintain their position. They established and promoted a corollary to the equalitarian creed, which held that the Negro was inferior, therefore excluding him from equal access and participation in American society. This corollary facilitated the formation of racial prejudicial attitudes. As Myrdal writes:

> The race dogma is nearly the only way out for a people so moralistically equalitarian, if it is not prepared to live up to its faith. A nation less fervently committed to democracy would, probably, live happily in a caste system with a somewhat less intensive belief in the biological inferiority of the subordinate group. The need for race prejudice is, from this point of view, a need for defense on the part of the Americans against their own national Creed, against their own most cherished ideals. And race prejudice is, in this sense, a function of equalitarianism. The former is a perversion of the latter.[9]

For example, a democratic principle is that all men have a right to participate in the democratic process, yet many feel that this is a right which should be denied to Negroes. The intervening "mechanism of rationalization" which reduces this inconsistency is the belief that "Negroes are innately less intelligent than whites," or that "Negroes are less well educated than whites," and therefore should be denied this right to participate in the democratic process. These mechanisms of rationalization may or may not be empirically

[9] *Ibid.*, p. 89.

true, but they are believed to be true and thus have the effect of reducing the discrepancy or inconsistency for individuals who subscribe to the contradictory beliefs.

The development of these prejudicial beliefs allowed most of white America to exclude the Negro from the benefits of an equalitarian society. If the Negro were inherently inferior, he need not be allowed a share: in fact, he is not entitled to a fair share. Racism functions to pervert equalitarianism.

Making these dogmas of inferiority thoroughly convincing required the development of biological and scientific 'proofs' of the differences between the races. Early investigations formulated various 'scientific' theories proving that, in fact, the races were not equal. Fortified with these proofs, the racist attitudes seemed justified. Myrdal notes:

Another accomplishment of early rationalistic Enlightenment has laid the theoretical basis for the racial defense of slavery; the recognition of *Homo sapiens* as only a species of the animal world and the emerging study of the human body and mind as biological phenomena. Until this philosophical basis was laid, racialism was not an intellectual possibility.[10]

The racist theories continued beyond the Enlightenment. As Myrdal continues:

The numerous enemies of the Negro left a whole crop of pseudoscientific writings in the libraries, emphasizing racial differences. Robert W. Shufeldt's book, *America's Greatest Problem: The Negro,* which had considerable influence for a time—illustrating the inferiority argument by a picture of a Negro lad between two monkeys and filled with an imposing mass of presumed evidences for Negro inferiority—is a late example of this literature at its worst.[11]

Only relatively recently in American history have these dogmas been systematically questioned. Valid scientific research has indicated the severe fallacies in arguments that the Negro is innately inferior. Myrdal had noted this new development:

From the vantage point of their present research front, the situation looks somewhat like this: a handful of social and biological scientists over the last fifty years have gradually forced informed people to give up some of the more blatant of our biological errors ...

Social research has thus become militantly critical. It goes from

[10] *Ibid.*
[11] *Ibid.*, p. 90.

discovery to discovery by challenging this basic assumption in various areas of life. It is constantly disproving inherent differences and explaining apparent ones in cultural and social terms. By inventing and applying ingenious specialized research methods, the popular race dogma is being victoriously pursued into every corner and effectively exposed as fallacious or at least unsubstantiated.[12]

Today it is an almost universally accepted fact that there are no inherent biological distinctions among races which outweigh cultural or social factors. And this evidence has shaken the myth of inferiority which for so long operated as a mechanism of rationalization.

The American Dilemma, as described by Myrdal, is directly relevant to the *New* American Dilemma that now confronts us, because resolution of Myrdal's dilemma—the prejudiced view of the Negro as inferior—underlies the crisis we now face. The relationship is a simple but brutal one: *The Negro has never been able to join a winning coalition because of the prejudice of the rest of the society*. Even in the few cases where the Negro might have found common ground in interests or memberships, especially with other minority groups, these other groups have been unwilling to join him out of fear, hatred, or feelings of superiority—all concomitants of their view of the Negro as inferior. Thus, for the Negro, the worst of all situations exists: he lives in a society based upon an assumption of competing groups and coalition formation. Yet, to become a part of a winning coalition, he must be a part of a social structure which enjoins him (on the basis of prejudice) from membership. For him, all cleavages in the society are reinforcing— against him. Except for his size as a group, white society as an invisible majority might forever dominate him at will, as it did in his earlier days by suppressing violently his suicidal insurrections and emasculating him from Reconstruction days until the early 1900's, and even as it has the American Indian.

The unsuccessful resolution of Myrdal's dilemma—namely, a prejudicial view of the Negro as still somehow inferior—underlies the New American Dilemma by forcing white America to again salve its conscience. While Americans have recently appeared more liberal in their thinking about the Negro, they have not become noticeably more liberal in their actions.

[12] *Ibid.*, p. 92.

Frank Westie,[13] in a study of Indianapolis in 1957, found evidence to support this ramification of the Myrdal thesis. First of all, respondents were more likely to agree with 'general valuation' statements about equality, democracy, and brotherhood than they were to parallel 'specific valuation' statements which applied to Negroes. Secondly, respondents tended to see that there was a contradiction between their general and specific responses. Thirdly, respondents tended to introduce additional intervening propositions which would 'explain' or 'account for' this contradiction.

Westie astutely notes that "We do not know (1) whether the conflict our respondents experienced in the interview exists for them outside the interview situation, or (2) whether it exists on an affective as well as a verbal or intellectual level."[14] We would suggest that this is a very important question if we are to understand the American public's response to the racial crisis in this nation.

Prior to the civil rights movement in America, the discrepancy in the contradictory values probably reached the cognitive level only infrequently for most Americans. But as the civil rights movement has drawn more and more attention to the realities of the Negro's condition in society, the awareness of this discrepancy in the cognitive process has begun to reach the surface with greater frequency. Similarly, scientific studies have made it increasingly difficult for educated Americans to explain away the discrepancies with the 'tried and true' rationalizations. Repeated studies have failed to confirm that Negroes are 'innately inferior.'

The reduction of this conflict has been achieved by a greater willingness on the part of the American public to acknowledge that the general valuations of freedom and equality also apply to Negroes. Thus, the public opinion polls show a marked trend in the proportion of Americans who believe that Negroes should have an equal opportunity to get ahead, equal educational opportunities, and the right to purchase a home that they can afford, etc. In one sense, this may represent real progress in breaking down the barriers of prejudice and discrimination. In another sense, however, this increasing 'liberalness' is occurring at a *gen-*

[13] Frank Westie, "The American Dilemma: An Empirical Test," *American Sociological Review*, Vol. 30, August, 1965, pp. 531–532.

[14] *Ibid.*, p. 538.

eral level, which serves to reduce the cognitive discrepancy between the principles held in the American Creed and the realities of the Negro condition in America, *but* the evidence does not support the contention that Americans are becoming significantly more liberal on *specific* valuations which involve the implementation of the general valuations. For example, public opinion polls indicate that an increasing proportion of Americans believe that Negroes are entitled to equal educational opportunities, but they do not support the contention that Americans are significantly more willing to have Negroes attend schools with *their* children. The polls indicate that an increasing proportion of Americans acknowledge that Negroes should have the right to purchase a home according to their economic means, but this does not mean that Americans are increasingly more willing to have a Negro as *their* neighbor.

Thus, at the general level, white Americans are willing to admit now that the doctrines of the American Creed dictate that the Negro *should* enjoy greater participation—in fact, equal participation in the American system—but the evidence does not indicate that they will act to insure that this happens.

The evidence suggests that the 'liberalness' of an attitudinal response on the race issue is a function of (1) the probability that the view expressed implies *direct interaction* with Negroes and (2) the *intensity* of the interaction implied. In other words, the greater the probability that intense interaction is implied by a value statement, the less willing are white Americans to agree with a liberal attitude statement. On the other hand, if the attitude statement suggests a low probability of interaction and the interaction implied is at a low level of intensity, the greater the likelihood of agreement with the statement.

Table 9 presents the twenty value statements from the Westie study with the general valuation on the left and the specific valuation on the right. In every case, a greater proportion of respondents agree with the general than with the specific valuation. But a more careful examination of the items suggests additional interpretations which are consistent with our contention that favorable civil rights attitudes are a function of the probability of interaction with Negroes, as well as the intensity of interaction.

TABLE 9

PERCENTAGE AGREEING WITH GENERAL
AND SPECIFIC VALUATION STATEMENTS

General Valuation Statement	Percentage Agreeing	Specific Valuation Statement	Percentage Agreeing
Everyone in America should have an equal opportunity to get ahead.	98	I would be willing to have a Negro as my supervisor in my place of work.	60
All people should be treated as equals in the eyes of the law.	98	If I went on trial I would not mind having Negroes on the jury.	76
Children should have equal educational opportunities.	98	I would not mind having Negro children attend the same school my children go to.	79
People should help each other in time of need.	99	If a Negro's home burned down, I would be willing to take his family into my home for the night.	64
Everyone should have equal right to hold public office.	91	I believe that I would be willing to have a Negro representative in the Congress of the United States.	71
Each person should be judged according to his own individual worth.	97	I would not mind if my children were taught by a Negro school teacher.	67
I believe in the principle of brotherhood among men.	94	I would be willing to invite Negroes to a dinner party in my home.	29
Public facilities should be equally available to everyone.	83	I would be willing to stay in a hotel that accommodates Negroes as well as whites.	61

TABLE 9—Continued

PERCENTAGE AGREEING WITH GENERAL
AND SPECIFIC VALUATION STATEMENTS

General Valuation Statement	Percentage Agreeing	Specific Valuation Statement	Percentage Agreeing
Under our democratic system people should be allowed to live where they please if they can afford it.	60	I would be willing to have a Negro family live next door to me.	35
I believe that all public recreational facilities should be available at all times.	63	I don't think I would mind if Negro children were to swim in the same pool as my children.	38

SOURCE: *Frank R. Westie, "The American Dilemma: An Empirical Test,"* American Sociological Review, *Vol. 30, August, 1965, pp. 531–532.*

The first three items in Table 9 deal with equal opportunities; equal opportunities to get ahead, equality before the law, and equal educational opportunities. Virtually everyone (98%) agrees with these statements. When the specific implications of these statements are presented, the proportion agreeing drops off significantly, but a substantial majority still agree with the specific statement (60–79%). Keeping in mind that this study was conducted in 1957, examination of the specific content of these items is suggestive of our thesis. Seventy-nine per cent, almost four-fifths, report that they would not object to having Negro children attend school with their children. Considering the turmoil that has erupted over school integration, this response seems like extremely liberal sentiment. But two important factors should be kept in mind. First, the data were gathered before school integration became a highly salient feature of American race relations. Secondly, Negroes in Indianapolis, as in most other American cities, are residentially segregated so that the possibility of school integration seemed rather remote. This was before bussing children to achieve integration had been discussed very seriously. Hence, removed from the possibility of this statement implying actual involvement or interaction with Negroes, it was relatively easy to agree with. The same is true for the statement regarding Negroes sitting on a jury before which they might be on trial. The vast majority of Americans have never been on trial, don't anticipate ever being on trial, and hence it is hard for them to realistically envision the hypothetical situation. As a result, three-quarters say they would not object. Having a Negro as a supervisor at work is a little more realistic for some persons, since they actually work with Negroes, and they are more hesitant to agree with the proposition than with the first two statements (60%). But, for the majority, the possibility of a Negro supervisor is rather remote, and hence agreement with the question is not too difficult.

The last two items in Table 9 demonstrate what happens to attitudes when interaction is implied. The general statements deal with housing and recreational facilities, two issues which at the time had some saliency for Indianapolis residents. On these items agreement with the general valuation statements (60% and 63%) falls below agreement with the first three *specific* valuations. It is not necessary to mention Negroes specifically in the general statements because these are issues where the *status quo* of the accommodative social structure has already been clearly challenged. Many respondents understand that agreement with the statement implies intense interaction with Negroes. When the context is made more specific (Negroes living next door and in the same swimming pool) the proportion agreeing drops off to a little more than one-third.

Perhaps the most revealing illustration of this thesis is found in item seven. Ninety-four per cent agree that they believe in the principle of brotherhood. For reasons which we need not analyze, Americans have long thought it appropriate to express brotherhood by periodic highly structured visitations. National Brotherhood Week is the prime example of a highly structured and culturally acceptable time for violating the normal accommodative structure by breaking bread together with persons of other ethnic, racial, or religious groups. While this usually occurs on 'neutral ground,' i.e., a public place, home visitation is also usually acceptable. Thus, the specific value statement, "I would be willing to invite Negroes to a dinner party in my home," is in keeping with the American tradition of expressing brotherhood. But notice what happens. Only 29 per cent assent to the proposition, the lowest proportion agreeing with any of the twenty statements.

What has happened? We would suggest that two factors account for this response. First, it implies a high degree of intimate interaction. Secondly, at this point in the interview the interviewee may question the credibility of the interviewer. The interviewer has explained that he is from the University of Indiana and that he is conducting research, but is he really? The interviewee may well be asking himself, "What happens if I say yes? Will I be asked to have Negroes into my home? Is this person really in my home under false pretenses?" In other words, this question implies a high degree of intimate interaction and it may well be *perceived* as a highly probable situation *vis a vis* the interviewer who is unknown to the respondent.

This may be reading too much into the contextual situation, but we don't believe that it is. We know that those who view their neighborhood as a target for integration are more opposed to integrated housing than those whose neighborhoods are 'safe' from integration. Before leaving the Westie data, it is informative to compare the response to the dinner invitation with the specific valuation of item four of Table 9. This item states "If a Negro's home burned down, I would be willing to take his family into my home for the night." Sixty-four per cent, or more than twice as many people, agree with this statement than agreed that they would be willing to invite a Negro to dinner. While 99 per cent of the respondents agreed that "People should help each other in time of need," we might legitimately ask why they should be so willing to help someone they wouldn't invite to dinner. The answer, we believe, rests in assessing the probability of the event occurring. In the first place, not very many people's homes burn down. Secondly, being residentially segregated from the Negroes, the probability that any individual white family would be asked to take a distressed Negro family in for the night is so remote as to be incalculable. Hence, while the level of interaction would be intimate, the probability of the event occurring is very, very low. Therefore, it is not extremely difficult for one to agree with the statement.

This analysis leads to a realization most of white America finds hard to accept. The granting of *de jure* equality will not result in

de facto gains *per se*. Even if whites are willing to grant (in principle) equality to Negroes, they will be far less willing to grant
equality in fact. This has been one of the major findings which
emerge from the civil rights movement. While it has been relatively
easy, by comparison, to gain *de jure* equality (and acceptance of
general valuations), it has also been much more difficult to gain *de
facto* equality (and acceptance of specific valuations). Thus while
the dispelling of the innately inferior racial concepts opened the
way for *de jure* gains, it by no means assured *de facto* advancement. On an intellectual level the dilemma of Myrdal is resolved—
the Negro must be a part of the equalitarian system. But on an
implementation level, there is still more than considerable opposition. White America has granted black America only tokens of
the improvements which black America feels it deserves.

Nonetheless, the now ambivalent resolution of Myrdal's dilemma
(ambivalent in the general-specific attitude conflicts which still
indicate high levels of specific prejudice) has had an enormous
impact. The Negro was able to utilize this argument to effect
important changes in the manner in which society deals with him.
The demonstration that the Negro was not innately inferior
dispelled in part (on the general level) the mechanism of rationalization which had permitted white America to continue a system
of caste subordination. Without this mechanism, the equalitarian
ethic demanded the Negro be allowed equal participation in the
system.

Such thinking provided the base for the 1954 Supreme Court
decision which demanded an end to "separate but equal." Since
1954, the Court as a conscience for the equalitarian ethic has
further extended *de jure* equality to the Negro. Yet it still remains
to translate the Court's attitudes to the American citizen. As time
has passed, some of the attitudes of whites have changed. But the
changes have occurred at the general, not the specific level. The
Negro is viewed more as an equal, but only so long as his equality
'keeps him away from me and my family.'

PATRONIZING REDRESS

This general-specific ambivalence of American whites has quag-
mired America into the depths of its New Dilemma. As the deplorable condition of the Negro continues, a few true liberals, a

large number of exploitive 'liberal' politicians, and a patronizing American public, desirous of 'keeping the Nigger in his place,' have joined together to 'give' Negroes *de jure* (and some *de facto*) opportunities for fuller participation in American society. Note that even here the Negro is not part of the winning coalition. His fate is, rather, decided upon by patronizing members of white society, some of which operate out of fear, some out of ignorance, and only a small number, if any, out of concern for the Negro.

IRONIC VIOLENCE

Unfortunately for the white 'winning coalition' its victory is Pyrrhic because the tokenism so begrudgingly given to the Negro is probably the key to his demand for complete participation in the society. The revolution of rising expectations applies to black Americans as well as white. America's entry into both World War I and World War II required Negro labor for the war efforts and created more conditions for the nation's New Dilemma: as the Negro gained some economic and social progress, his aspirations and his expectations rose. Each time the Negro asserted these aspirations, he was met with white resistance, often in the form of violence. But the spark had been fanned and was not to be extinguished. As we indicated earlier, at this point in the developing pattern of race relations the spark of aspirations sometimes fanned also into the full flame of black-dominated violence.

In the 1960's, several historic events raised Negro aspirations and expectations higher than at any other time—aspirations for a better share of the 'goodies' and expectations that the ability to achieve those aspirations was near at hand. Other events, however, seem to have been perceived by the Negro as abruptly retarding his progress.

Heading the list of events causing hopes and expectations to rise was the ascendance to fame and leadership of the late Dr. Martin Luther King. King's successful attack, at least on *de jure* discrimination in the South, aroused new hopes in Negro America for self-betterment. The election of John Kennedy, a liberal white, probably fanned the flames of this aroused sentiment as Kennedy's sympathy for the Negro cause became apparent in his proposals for civil rights legislation. Although Kennedy introduced civil

rights legislation, he was unable to pass it. But Lyndon Johnson—
capitalizing on the nation's feeling for the martyrized President—
was able to railroad the Congress into the passage of three historic civil rights laws.

The hopes aroused by these developments were probably sufficient to create, both in myth and in some actual improvement, an
expectation on the part of the Negro that his state in life would
improve. The final cause of this rising level of expectation came
with the first onslaughts of the last five summers of violence: the
goals that the Negro sought to fulfill began to be perceived by
Negroes as possible through violent action, once the first summer
of rioting occurred and was met with remedial (token though it
was) reaction by the white communities involved.

Another factor, which crystallized the Negro's generalized belief, was probably the *perception* (most likely untrue) that certain
situations were abruptly retarding his desired progress. We say
that this perception was most probably untrue for two reasons:
(a) it is doubtful that any rapid gains were really being made
toward Negro progress, and (b) those situations generally identified as the causes of abrupt retardation of rapid progress probably really had little effect on that progress.

In the first instance, we are referring to the reality that real
progress for the Negro meant breaking the barriers of *de facto*
segregation, for without success in the bread-and-butter, jobs,
homes, and votes issues, the Negro could not really achieve significant progress. Token integration of schools, busses, and lunch-
counters simply is not significant in the long run. And this is just
about all the Negro has achieved to this point.

In the second instance, the primary situation perceived as cause
for the abrupt retardation of progress—namely, the Vietnam War
—probably has had little impact on the nation's program to improve the Negro's lot. Despite the fact that war costs have soared,
the amounts of money allocated to the nation's poor have increased
far above levels most persons would have thought possible a few
years ago. Even while we increased our nation's expenditures in
Vietnam to over $25 billion a year, war-on-poverty programs in-
creased by over 25 per cent in total Federal funding. (The war
has, however, resulted in cutbacks since 1967.) To assume that an
early settlement of the Vietnam conflict would have resulted in

the definite rechanneling of greater resources to fight poverty and improve the life chances of the Negro is probably unwarranted. There are too many interest groups standing in line waiting to get a piece of the federal monies and too many white Americans who think that the Negro has already received too generous a proportion of federal expenditures. Thus, Vietnam is probably irrelevant.

In any case, this factor—the perception that certain situations are causing retardation in the Negro's progress—has another (and probably more crucial) aspect: white resistance to the improvement of the lot of the American Negro. Probably resulting both from ignorance and outright prejudice, most whites do not mind the abstract improvements planned and implemented for Negro America, but they do resist the practical applications of those abstractions.

THE NEW AMERICAN DILEMMA

The irony of the New American Dilemma, then, is that it results from our unsuccessful attempt to escape the resolution of the old American Dilemma. We have become a people hypocritical in the distinction we make between the Negro's theoretical or general right to full participation in our society and the practical or specific applications of those theoretical rights. As a consequence, we have attempted to salve our consciences concerning the deplorable condition of the American Negro through ineffective tokenism. But our self-ruse has backfired—in a two-fold manner: not only are Negroes not satisfied with our tokens and now shouting (and burning and shooting) for *de facto* gains, but their so-doing has reawakened, reaffirmed, and redisplayed the very bigotry we were trying to hide from ourselves.

The resurfacing of latent bigoted attitudes is compounded by a prejudice-motivated desire to suppress the Negro rather than to allocate the necessary and sufficient resources to obviate his protests. For white America, it has always been easier, faster, and more desirable to pass such legislation as an anti-riot bill than to take constructive action that would eliminate the underlying causes of disorder.

Once again white America is asserting itself in a manner which unwittingly exposes the prime manifestation of its consensual philosophy's underlying weakness: the inaccessibility of the system to its largest minority group. This inaccessibility merits further analysis, as the horns of the New American Dilemma begin to appear.

Myrdal's dilemma was an intellectual problem. It was largely a problem only to white America. The new dilemma is more than an intellectual problem—it is central to actual objective change and gain. Its ramifications not only plague white America—they pose a dilemma for black Americans as well. As we write this book in the late 1960's, the dilemma's horns are only beginning to take shape. But one thing is certain—the dilemma will continue to grow in importance. The final resolution of the dilemma—by both white and Negro Americans—may well shape the pattern of U. S. interracial relations for decades to come.

As we have noted, the democratic process in the United States functions on a pluralistic base. The system is organized so that majority rule decides important questions of policy. Even on an administrative level, the question of majority choice is relevant. A President finds it extremely difficult to make decisions which will not meet with majority approval. Hence the obsession with public opinion polls—the desire to know what the American people think of policy decisions. This fact of political life necessitates that groups wishing change within the democratic process formuate effective coalitions to gain objectives. Supported by a grouping of forces, a course of action is likely to become policy. The Negro then must formulate an effective coalition if he is to become effective within the democratic process. However, as we have noted, it is at this point that prejudice creates enormous difficulties.

A parallel to the Negro situation is available. The immigrant groups in the United States were faced with a similar problem. To gain social and economic acceptance in the American system they had to function politically. An important study of ethnic group behavior in such a situation is that of New York ethnic groups by Nathan Glazer and Daniel Patrick Moynihan, *Beyond the Melting Pot*. Glazer and Moynihan note that to gain desired objectives, ethnic groups found it a necessity to function as "interest groups"—i.e., groups of individuals bound by common and accepted interests:

... someone who is Irish or Jewish or Italian generally has other traits than the mere existence of the name that associates him with other people attached to the group. A man is connected to his group by ties of family and friendship. But he is also connected by ties of *interest*. The ethnic groups in New York are also *interest groups*.[15]

Thus, the individuals within these groups are bound by more than national backgrounds which are similar—they are joined by common objectives and interests. Glazer and Moynihan also pointed out that an individual of one group can attach himself to other groups when it is to his advantage to do so:

Under certain circumstances, strange as it may appear, it is an advantage to be able to take on a group name, even of a low order, if it can be made to fit, and if it gives one certain advantages. It is better in Oakland, California, to be a Mexican than an Indian, and so some of the few Indians call themselves, at certain times, for certain occasions, "Mexicans." In the forming of ethnic groups subtle distinctions are overridden; there is an advantage to belonging to a big group, even if it is looked down upon. West Indian Negroes achieve important political positions, as representatives of Negroes; Spaniards and Latin Americans become the representatives of Puerto Ricans; German Jews rose to Congress from districts dominated by East European Jews.[16]

This process of group coalition and group identification on the basis of interests is obviously more important when a group is a disadvantaged minority. At the initial stages of its emergence, such a coalition, even with other groups which are looked down upon can be essential to obtaining desired progress. However, after the initial stages, the second process of assimilation into the larger society takes place. Thus, second and third generation Irish or Italians gradually become less identified and dominated by their ethnic backgrounds and become more and more identified with general American norms and patterns of behavior.

This is not to say that their ethnic background is forgotten or not called upon when it is to their advantage; but these second and third generation ethnics find that assimilation into the mainstream of American life offers more potential for gain than the retention of their ethnic individuality. For many such Americans

[15] Nathan Glazer and Daniel P. Moynihan, *Beyond the Melting Pot: The Negroes, Puerto Ricans, Jews, Italians, and Irish of New York City* (Cambridge, Massachusetts: The MIT Press, 1963), p. 17.

[16] *Ibid.*, pp. 16–17.

ethnic background becomes largely unconscious. It is no longer the central factor of their outlook. They are first American and second Irish or Italian. Yet the assimilation, as Glazer and Moynihan note, never becomes complete. Ethnic background is still a relevant factor in a predominately white, Anglo-Saxon, and Protestant nation.

The Negro finds himself in a distinct position. He finds it exceedingly difficult to formulate an effective coalition. First, most of the other ethnic and racial groups, who were once as disadvantaged as the Negro is currently, have made sufficient progress to no longer identify their problems with those of the Negro. In addition, for a variety of reasons, these recently assimilated groups seem to be the most overt in their expressions of a prejudiced viewpoint toward the Negro. Thus, he is universally cast aside by one recognizable factor—his race.

The formation of a coalition—even if other ethnic groups with similar interests did exist—becomes very difficult. The factor of race adds the greatest element of complexity: the Negro finds it more difficult to enter—i.e., assimilate—into American society. In a color-conscious society, the Negro is kept a distinct minority. Even those Negroes who do attempt assimilation find that the fact of their color keeps them apart and separate. Unable to formulate coalitions with other ethnic minorities with similar interests, and unable to assimilate, the Negro finds it difficult to amass the power base needed to effectively express himself in a democratic process which expects coalitions to arise out of the pluralistic society.

Another relevant factor is that some Negroes—perhaps in response to the reality of their inability to formulate a coalition—have begun to reject whites as well as Negroes who are not firmly committed to the black community. This is the logic of black power and black nationalism. Many Negroes want to fight their crusade alone. They don't want the cooperation and participation of whites. They want their drive for equality to be Negro-led and Negro-dominated. This is the rationale groups like the Congress of Racial Equality (CORE) have underlying their going 'all-black' in the summer of 1967. Such a feeling on the part of the Negro can exclude the possibility of establishing the type of coalition necessary for a minority to win its point in a democratic society. The Negro, trying to go it alone, determines that he will continue to function as a minority and significantly reduces his opportunity to play the game of pluralistic democracy successfully.

Yet, we must question the efficacy of the democratic process for black Americans. Assuming the Negro could amass a coalition and continue to press forward through the democratic process, would there be any significant gains? Perhaps not. Gunnar Myrdal observed the questionable place of law in the United States. The passage of a law does not necessarily result in behavior according to that law. We have already noted several violent and unlawful American traditions. One tradition which Myrdal noted was that Americans reserve the right to determine for themselves whether to obey a law or not. Prohibition and gambling laws failed because Americans decided not to obey them. There was a stronger commitment to the behavior such laws prohibited than there was a commitment to the idealistic justification which prompted their enactment. Furthermore, Myrdal noted that the tradition has been for American law to be haphazardly enacted and even more haphazardly enforced.[17] Congressmen formulate laws in many spheres of activity—many areas where they are not specialists. At times it takes too much effort—or the noncompliance is too general to obtain total obedience to a law. So the passage of legislation in the United States has never assured behavior patterns which conform to the hopes of the legislators.

This has been the situation of the American Negro. We have noted that the Negro has won *de jure* recognition: at the same time we emphasized that the objective realities of the Negro's situation in the U. S. have not significantly improved—even with the passage of civil rights legislation, reinforced by judicial decisions.

Let us examine school desegregation as a specific example. The 1954 Supreme Court decision was cited as the key to opening the movement for *de jure* recognition. Yet the objective reality of schooling in the United States remains the rule of segregation. As Martin Gansberg of the *New York Times* pointed out in January of 1968:

Despite efforts of some governmental leaders, educators, and civic groups, desegregation has not kept up with growth of the school

[17] Myrdal, *op. cit.*, especially pp. 15–23.

population. There are now 2.5 million Negro children in all-Negro
public schools; before the 1954 Supreme Court decision ordering an
end to school segregation there were 2.2 million ...

The problem of de facto segregation is particularly acute in large
cities, where 75 percent of Negro elementary students attend schools
with enrollments that are nearly all-Negro.[18]

At this point, let us make it perfectly clear that other minorities
have not been altogether successful in their attempts to advance
through the democratic process. An Irish Catholic may have been
elected President of the United States, but it is still impossible
for many first, second, and third generation ethnics to live in
certain places or to obtain certain jobs. There are still limits to
the opportunities available to an Italian, an Irishman, or a Jew.
We only wish to indicate that the difficulties facing the Negro are
enormously more complex. Even his opportunity for cooperation
with ethnic groups is reduced. His chance of gains such as were
won by the ethnics—even though these gains have not been complete—are significantly more difficult than they were for the
ethnics.

The reality of the situation is that the democratic process offers
less chance of success for the Negro both in terms of joining a
coalition which can continue to produce legislation and in terms
of gaining the willingness of a society to comply with any legislation that is passed. And some laws have been passed, but they
have made little difference in the life of the slum dweller. The
laws which could make a significant difference have not been
passed. If they were, it is questionable whether they would be complied with.

THE HORNS OF THE NEGRO'S DILEMMA

The Negro in his drive for implementation of *de facto* equality
faces a choice: he can attempt to effect change through the established democratic process or he can resort to violence. In either
case, the prospect is not optimistic. The dilemma is that neither
road to equality is likely to produce the desired change.

[18] Martin Gansberg, "Integration: The Gap Is Widening," *New York
Times*, January 12, 1968, p. 49. © 1968 by the New York Times Company.
Reprinted by permission.

Proponents of Black Power implicitly recognize their race's inability to join into a winning coalition to achieve significant gains. They go so far as to damn white liberals who have identified with the Negro cause—and often with good justification, because many of the so-called liberals have merely used the Negro for their own purposes. Men like Stokely Carmichael and H. Rap Brown see the necessity for black unity, because they realize the impossibility of gaining really effective non-black support. Since the system has for so long denied Negroes the opportunity to join a winning coalition, Negroes must go it alone and join together to form their own winning coalition.

That an all-Negro coalition cannot achieve the goals of its members (because, even were significant legislation passed, which is not likely, it is more unlikely that it would be observed or enforced) is also implicitly recognized by men like Carmichael and Brown. Their advocacy of violence would be unnecessary if the Negro coalition could win significant victories in the legislative arena which would be translated into significant social gains.

The seeming ambivalence of a call for Negro unity to form a winning coalition and a simultaneous call for violence reflects the underlying sinister logic of Black Power. That logic is based on an understanding of the process of change of our society, which comes too close to the truth for the comfort of most of us. As an example: when *The Other America*[19] hit the commercial market in 1962, that part of American society which constitutes the other half of "The Other" was shocked, dismayed, and disgusted—but only briefly. Americans, as we have noted, have an amazing ability to become quickly disturbed and then to become even more quickly complacent.

Persons and agencies in control of the mechanisms in our society which satisfy the demands of its various competing groups are not much more moved than the general populace by *disturbing* situations until those situations become *crises* which continuously impinge upon their consciousness or, more likely, directly threaten their own well-being. For this reason, and for the reason that obedience to laws is not a singularly prominent American trait,

[19] Michael Harrington, *The Other America: Poverty in the United States* (New York: The Macmillan Company, 1963).

major social changes, as we have seen, do not occur in this nation without rancorous outbursts of hostility.

In this regard, it is interesting to note the comparative failure of Dr. King's programs in the North, as compared to their success in the South. Admitting all of the dissimilarities between the two situations, it is still true that one major reason for his failure in the North rests with his inability to bring the constant, crisis-type pressure on the power structures in northern communities that his nonviolent tactics achieved in the South. It may be precisely because the situations are totally dissimilar that his failure was so blatant: i.e., there may be a lower threshold of response in southern communities because the total number of factors impinging upon the consciousness of the power structure there is lower than the number of factors vying for the attention of the power structure in the more highly sophisticated industrial communities of the North. Or it may be that the power structure in the North is more insulated than that in the South by its very size or by its relatively greater complexity. It is also, of course, possible that we are here making a grand overestimation of King's success in the South; for it may be argued that the Negro's lot there has not been markedly improved.

Even if the governmental leaders wanted to eliminate or ameliorate the deprived status of the Negro, they could not do so unless support among their constituencies could be developed using the constituents' fear that continued violence might be directed at them and their institutions. Dr. Kenneth Clark, a noted Negro social scientist, has made the point succinctly:

Ideals alone ... do not bring justice. Ideals, combined with necessity, may.[20]

And there is empirical evidence to support this proposition:

While the gap between Negroes and whites in regard to the pace of change, and the cause and prevention of riots is quite large, the attitude of whites seems to be based on *ignorance* of or *indifference* (emphasis added) to the factual basis of Negro resentment and bitterness.

[20] Kenneth B. Clark, "The Dilemma of Power," introduction to Kenneth B. Clark and Talcott Parsons (editors), *The Negro American* (Boston: Houghton Mifflin Company, 1966), p. xviii.

Though disliking violence and troubled with mixed feelings about its effects, Negroes are shifting to the opinion that *only intense forms of social protest can bring relief from social injustice* (emphasis added). Negroes and whites agree that riots have produced some long-delayed action by city governments to increase opportunities for Negroes.[21]

The story of *The Other America,* told in many different ways, aided in the passage of a War on Poverty program. But that war program, as we have noted, has produced little in the way of improvement for the majority of Negroes. Instead, the condition of the ghetto Negro seems to be getting worse. A law was passed. But the law did not make any real changes. Had significant changes occurred, white America would have felt the pangs of far higher taxes or fear of a new Negro neighbor. And, had that happened, white America might not have complied with the law, unless it believed that noncompliance would have meant the likelihood of a home in flames or a bullet through the chest.

Indeed, then, perhaps the Black Power advocates understand better than most whites that Americans have traditionally paid only lip-service to their notion of consensus when critical issues arose; that, in fact, when critical issues arise, they can no longer be solved through the normal political channels based on common understandings; that, indeed, the only common interest a challenging minority and an unresponsive majority have is violence, with the minority offering peace only when the majority makes the requisite concessions.

However, for the Negro, the crushing blow is the unlikelihood that even violence will produce the attitude change necessary to permit him the progress he demands. As is the case with legislation based on 'moral' considerations, violence is unlikely to produce significantly desirable attitude changes. A study of white reactions to the Los Angeles Riot of 1965 shows that:

The most important factor in determining the reaction of whites to the disturbance appears to be their more basic attitudes toward Negroes. Respondents who are relatively antagonistic toward Negroes tend to view the riots as the result of outside 'agitation,' to believe the riots hurt the Negro's cause, and to suggest punitive solutions

[21]Lemberg Center for the Study of Violence, Brandeis University, *Six City Study* (unpublished report, June, 1967), p. 22.

to the problem. Conversely, respondents who are tolerant in their general attitudes toward Negroes tend to see the causes of the riots in such sources as white prejudice and discrimination against Negroes or lack of employment and educational opportunities, and more likely to believe the riots helped the Negro's cause, and are more likely to suggest ameliorative solutions to the problem, such as full civil rights for Negroes and increased educational and economic opportunities.[22]

Hence, the majority reaction to the riot was to reinforce prejudices and to justify antagonisms rather than to effect attitude changes. Note the further findings of the study.

In characterizing the events of August 11–15 [the dates of the Watts riots], its causes and its purpose, about a third of the white respondents showed some sympathy toward the disturbance.

Nineteen per cent stated that it helped and 74 per cent said it hurt the Negro cause.

Seventy-three per cent stated that it had increased the gap between the races, and 13 per cent stated it had decreased the gap.

Over half the whites felt some fear or a great deal of fear.

Nearly one-third considered using firearms, over one-half approved of buying guns, and some 12 per cent either bought or already had firearms.

Roughly one-third of the whites had an exaggerated idea of the size of the disturbance and the number of Negroes supporting it (even after three months of factual reports on the riot).

Some 20 per cent felt that the best way to prevent further riots was to take punitive or restrictive action of one form or another.[23]

While the riots did little to decrease the degree to which whites in general felt that Negroes were entitled to gains, it reinforced the specific valuations that Negroes should not be given gains if they would involve real concessions on the part of whites:

On measures of stereotypes and beliefs about racial differences; social distance questions; and attitudes of dislike and distrust of Negroes; and attitudes about Negro efforts to improve their position through social action; the findings were that: (a) The least amount of antagonism is found with regard to stereotypes, racial beliefs, and impersonal social relations, (b) while most antagonism is in the areas of social action programs and close social relationships.[24]

[22] Nathan E. Cohen, *Los Angeles Riot Study* (a preliminary report by the Director of the Los Angeles Riot Study group at UCLA, August, 1967), p. 9.
[23] *Ibid.*, pp. 8–9.
[24] *Ibid.*, p. 9.

In this regard, it is interesting to note the reaction of Congress
after the riots of 1967. Congress did not intensify efforts to improve poverty programs or other efforts aimed at satisfying some
of the demands made by Negroes. No more money was poured into
the ghettos. Rather, the Congress became disenchanted with the
poverty program efforts and reduced its appropriations. The demands of the Negroes were thus frustrated even more. Congress
merely demonstrated that its prejudices were also reinforced. One
of the most seriously considered (and passed) pieces of legislation
was not for more jobs or better houses, or greater health or
welfare benefits, but anti-riot legislation. With the second option,
violence, the Negro once again stands little chance of gaining
what he wants in terms of a *de facto* equality of results.

THE HORNS OF THE WHITE'S DILEMMA

As indicated previously, the Negro's assumption of an assertive
position has resulted in his directing the course of interracial
relations. Thus, the demand of the Negro for equality has put the
white American in a position of response. The optimum Negro
position from the white American's standpoint would be a position
of nonviolence. Perhaps some white Americans would prefer that
the Negro regress back to his mild assertiveness before the pressure for *de jure* rights. However, the Negro assertion and demand
for equality is a fact. In this context, the nonviolent tactic would
certainly be preferable to most white Americans. Nonviolence
would allow white America to slip back into complacency. But
violence is here, and white America must respond positively or
negatively. Neither option is realistic in terms of its implications
or results. With a positive response, the white American would
suddenly 'turn good,' i.e., he would realize the validity of the
Negro's claims and give him the *de facto* results he is demanding.
However, in view of the continuing prejudice demonstrated on
the specific valuation level, the option seems unrealistic. It seems
totally impossible that overnight the white American will suddenly
grant to the Negro what he wants in terms of housing, employment, education, etc. Whether the Negro chooses the nonviolent
approach or violence, white attitudes are unlikely to undergo a

rapid metamorphosis. At least for the present, white America is
unlikely to choose this positive response.

A negative response is far more probable. The loud applause
given the President's statement on street crime during his January,
1968, State of the Union Address, certainly demonstrated this likelihood. Such a response may entail increasing prejudices and fears
of the Negro. They could occur as a reaction to aggressive attempts
to make gains through the democratic process, or as a reaction to
violence on the Negro's part. This could involve not only intensifi-
cation of prejudices on the specific valuation level but might even
entail some reconsideration of general valuations. These valuations
are precisely what the Negro must cultivate for peaceful progress.
A reversion to more prejudicial positions by whites (because of
intensified Negro activity) would be likely to only intensify the
Negro's feeling that he must step up these activities.

But another type of negative response is possible. This involves
large-scale white paralysis, or the granting of only temporary or
token gains. Such a response, while basically attempting to maintain the *status quo*, could easily lead to chaos. The Negro will still
not have gained that which he seeks, and the escalation of Negro
pressure for real gains seems inevitable. (What we are primarily
concerned with here is the response of the majority. As we have
indicated before with regard to the Negro 'community,' a fragmented approach is likely. The same applies to whites.) There is
unlikely to be a consensus over the particular method the Negroes
decide to use; likewise, there is unlikely to be consensus over the
white response. However, what the majority does or is perceived to
be doing is likely to be interpreted as the response of all whites
or all Negroes and is likely to be responded to by the opposite
race as if the perception of what all members of the other race is
doing is a valid perception. Regardless of which negative option the
white community seems to be taking, it is unlikely that this option
will reduce the chance that violence will continue. The positive
option is unlikely; the negative options are self-defeating in that
they encourage the Negro to intensify his campaign for equality.
The direction in which he is moving and is, indeed, being pushed
by white society, is gravely dangerous for black and white alike.

chapter seven

A TIME TO BURN?

On March 1, 1968, the National Advisory Commission on Civil Disorders, appointed by President Johnson following the 1967 Detroit riot, issued its final report.[1] Those who thought that the Commission would succumb to political pressure and issue a 'whitewash' which failed to detail the magnitude of America's racial problem had miscalculated. The tone of the Commission's report was surprisingly strong, and the conclusion, while obvious to some, shocked many: "Our nation is moving toward two societies, one black, one white—separate and unequal." The Commission felt that if the nation continued to pursue its present course, discrimination and segregation would deepen the division between the races and intensify the polarization of the American community. The report was quick to point out that the alternatives were not only "blind repression" or "capitulation to lawlessness." A third alternative was endorsed: a "compassionate, massive and sustained" commitment to national action backed by the resources of the most powerful and richest nation on earth, accompanied by "new attitudes, new understanding and above all new will" from all Americans.

But the Commission went further, and in so doing, probably, even if unintentionally, intensified the polarization. Much of the blame for the destructive environment created in the Negro ghetto

[1] National Advisory Commission on Civil Disorders. *Report* (Washington, D. C.: U. S. Government Printing Office, 1968). Also known as the "Kerner Report" after its chairman, Otto Kerner, then governor of Illinois.

by segregation and poverty was laid at the doorstep of white America:

What white Americans have never fully understood—but what the Negro can never forget—is that white society is deeply implicated in the ghetto. White institutions created it, white institutions maintain it, and white society condones it.[2]

Regardless of the truth of the accusation or the sincerity with which it was made by the Commission, the overwhelming majority of white Americans, from the President on down, refused to accept the judgment. The report was greeted with a thundering silence from the White House. Many public officials and most white Americans, refusing to accept the label of "white racist," criticized and rejected it. The Commission can perhaps be faulted for not distinguishing between the more blatant forms of racism and those subtle forms which are practiced by so many.[3] The fact remains, however, that more than a year after the release of the Commission's report little or nothing has been done to implement its blueprint for remedial action. Black America has failed to communicate its message to white society even after violent and widespread protest and the assistance of a sympathetic analysis by a presidential commission.

Indeed, we must conclude that events since the report of the Kerner Commission have significantly increased, rather than decreased, the degree of polarization in American society. The alienation and anger of the black community and its protest against injustice, powerlessness and paralysis has spread to other parts of society and a 'crisis of authority' has developed rapidly. Legitimacy and relevance are being questioned not only in the cities, but also in the national government, in the political parties, in the churches, and on college and high school campuses.

The year 1968 was one of the most dramatic periods of civil violence in American history. The scope, variety and intensity of violence and violence-related events occurring during the year, interpreted in the light of past experience (as developed in the

[2] *Ibid.*, p. 1.
[3] For a discussion of this distinction, see Jeffrey K. Hadden, "The Riots Report: A Glaring Omission," *Commonweal* (March 29, 1968); and T. M. Tomlinson, "White Racism and the Common Man: An Extension of the Kerner Commission's Report on American Racism" (mimeo), 1968.

preceding chapters), may offer some insight into potential future developments and alternatives. What conclusions can be drawn from the significant events of the immediate past such as the publication and response to the Kerner Commission report, the violence in the streets of Chicago during the Democratic convention, the assassinations of Martin Luther King, Jr. and Robert F. Kennedy, two major national figures in the battle for justice and equality, the 'shoot-out' in Cleveland between black nationalists and police, the presidential campaign and its emphasis on 'law and order,' the deteriorating relationship between Jews and Negroes, the further development of black power, black separatism, and community control, the growing concern with irresponsible police behavior, and the rapidly accelerating crisis of the campus? Are they to be evaluated as separate events, or do they, perhaps, in combination suggest the direction in which the nation is moving?

A YEAR OF POLARIZING VIOLENCE

The pattern of racial violence after 1963, which we have characterized as Negro-dominated, property-oriented violence, appeared to peak in 1968 following the assassination of Martin Luther King, Jr. in Memphis. The timing was ironic. The assassination came only one month after the National Advisory Commission on Civil Disorders had blamed "white racism" for most of the urban violence of the preceding four years. During the two weeks following the assassination there were more than one hundred riots across the nation resulting in more than forty deaths. They ranged from relatively minor incidents to major disruptions in Chicago, Baltimore and Washington, D. C. The April violence appeared to be an almost spontaneous reaction of angry black people throughout the nation to a national tragedy which symbolized the murder of a black hero by white America.

The violence of 1968 shifted from cities to campuses and from black to white following the pervasive outbreaks after the King assassination. The presidential campaign of 1968 provided the framework for the two major violent events after April: the assassination of Senator Robert F. Kennedy in Los Angeles on June 4, the night of his dramatic primary victory in California, and the week of violence on the streets of Chicago during the Democratic national convention in August. Neither event involved Negroes in any significant way. The man convicted of the shooting of Robert Kennedy is a Syrian, presumably distraught by Kennedy's strong support of Israel in the continuing Middle East struggle. The street violence of Chicago, which is often referred to as the "Battle of Chicago," pitted white police and guardsmen against a coalition of almost all white anti-war protest groups. (Indeed, Chicago's large contingent of militant blacks was conspicuous in its absence.) As millions watched on television, Chicago police savagely and brutally beat protest marchers, members of the press, and even innocent bystanders. A report on the Chicago violence requested by the President's National Commission on the Causes and Prevention of Violence,[4] and written by a respected Chicago lawyer-businessman, Daniel Walker, concluded that "although the Chicago police were the targets of mounting provocation by both word and act ... the nature of the response was unrestrained and indiscriminate police violence ...":[5]

That violence was made all the more shocking by the fact that it was often inflicted upon persons who had broken no law, disobeyed no order, made no threat. These included peaceful demonstrators, onlookers, and large numbers of residents who were simply passing through, or happened to live in, the areas where confrontations were occurring.[6]

That some policemen lost control of themselves under exceedingly provocative circumstances can perhaps be understood; but not con-

---

[4] This Commission, appointed by President Johnson on June 6, 1968, immediately after the assassination of Senator Kennedy, was the second national violence commission in less than a year. Its predecessor, the National Advisory Commission on Civil Disorders, had issued its report only three months earlier. The new Commission's scope was considerably broader than the first one, including political assassination and other forms of personal violence, as well as another investigation of civil violence. Critics of the Violence Commission, notably Arthur Schlesinger, Jr., were concerned about its composition which included a Senatorial spokesman for the National Rifle Association (Roman Hruska), but no representatives of alienated groups, "no scholars, no scientists, not even a representative of labor." See Arthur Schlesinger, Jr., *Violence: America in the Sixties* (New York: Signet, 1968), p. 48.

[5] Daniel Walker, *Rights in Conflict* (The Violent Confrontation of Demonstrators and Police in the Parks and Streets of Chicago During the Week of the Democratic National Convention of 1968). A Report to the National Commission on the Causes and Prevention of Violence, November 18, 1968., p. vii.

[6] *Ibid.*

doned. If no action is taken against them, the effect can only be to discourage the majority of policemen who acted responsibly, and further weaken the bond between the police and community.[7]

There has been no public condemnation of these violators of 'sound police procedures' by either their commanding officers or city officials. In fact Mayor Richard Daley went to great lengths to defend the behavior of his police force, and indirectly, himself. In a statement to the delegates of the Democratic national convention on August 29, 1968, Mayor Daley argued that it was his responsibility "to protect the delegates and the people of Chicago from this planned violence."[8] He admitted that "in the heat of emotion and riots some police may have over-reacted," but he asserted that the entire police force should not be judged on the alleged actions of a few. He insisted that his administration had never condoned brutality at any time, but neither would it ever "permit a lawless violent group of terrorists to menace the lives of millions of people, destroy the purpose of [a] national political convention, and take over the streets of Chicago."[9] In Chicago's April riot, a strategy of restraint employed by the superintendent of police had been countermanded by the mayor who ordered the police to "shoot to kill arsonists and shoot to maim looters."

The Daley defense was a major job of city public relations. City Hall prepared and circulated a lengthy and detailed report entitled "The Strategy of Confrontation," and televised a one-hour documentary criticizing the protesters and defending the mayor and police in an effort to compensate for what Daley considered the biased coverage of the events by national news media.

Order was restored in Chicago. As the mayor pointed out: "The convention was not disrupted; the city was not paralyzed. Not one shot was fired; not one life lost." Indeed, order was restored in Chicago, but at what cost to ultimate domestic peace?

What is perhaps more disturbing than the Chicago street battle itself is the public opinion expressed. Results of a Gallup poll taken the week after the convention show that fifty-six per cent of those polled approved of the way the Chicago police had dealt with the youthful protesters while only thirty-one per cent dis-

[7] *Ibid.*, p. xiii.
[8] Quoted in the *New York Times*, August 30, 1968, p. 1.
[9] *Ibid.*

approved.[10] Among Negroes, who until the Chicago battle had been the prime targets of police violence, sixty-three per cent *disapproved* of police tactics and only eighteen per cent approved, compared with twenty-nine per cent and fifty-nine per cent respectively among whites. Apparently white public opinion tends to support the use of force against protesters regardless of their color. Perhaps the generation gap is as wide as the racial gap.

Although the King and Kennedy assassinations and the Chicago battle represent the major violent events of 1968 (the response to the Kerner report must rate as the major *non-event* of the year), there were others. There were more riots and disorders during the first eight months of 1968 (313) than during the entire year of 1967 (164), the worst previous riot year, more property damage ($78 million to $67 million), and only eleven fewer riot deaths (78 compared with 89). Figures compiled by the U. S. Department of Justice and the Lemberg Center for the Study of Violence (Brandeis University) indicate that only forty per cent of the 1968 civil disorders can be accounted for by the rioting following the King assassination.

The pattern of ghetto violence and response seemed to change significantly in 1968. The post-April rioting, although widespread, was smaller in scale, and more quickly suppressed. City officials and police seem to have learned something from their riot experiences during the preceding four summers. They reacted more quickly and firmly to suppress violence without using unnecessary force in most instances. The post-King riots themselves, widespread simultaneous rioting precipitated by a single event of national import, represented a significant departure from the successive city-by-city pattern in previous summers.

There was still another, and perhaps more significant development in the pattern of urban violence during 1968. In a number of cities, black militants engaged in direct gunfire attacks on police (as opposed to previous sporadic sniping during or after looting and burning). At least eight policemen died and forty-seven others were seriously wounded. Of the cities where this took place—Cincinnati, New York, Seattle, Peoria, Gary, and Cleveland—the so-called 'shoot-out' in Cleveland on July 23 was the most intense and probably the most significant. In a five-hour gun

[10] *New York Times*, September 18, 1968.

battle on the evening of July 23 ten persons were killed, including three policemen and three black militants. The incident received considerable attention for two reasons: (1) the mayor of Cleveland, Carl B. Stokes, is black, and (2) he employed the somewhat unorthodox strategy of removing white policemen and National Guardsmen from the black community for twenty-four hours and inserting an all-black Mayor's Committee to restore order and prevent further bloodshed. Although no one was killed following the implementation of this strategy, the police and ghetto businessmen who suffered extensive looting and fire bombing severely criticized Stokes.[11]

The question raised by this series of apparently premeditated attacks on the police is, of course, whether a new pattern of guerrilla warfare designed to inflict death and injury to *persons* might be replacing the former pattern of *property-oriented* ghetto violence.

And person-oriented violence has not been confined to black militants; the police have also used it. This, along with other criticisms of police behavior, has begun to seriously undermine the confidence of the public and public officials in the ability of the police, as currently organized and trained, to provide fair, impartial, and effective public safety for all citizens, black and white. In a report prepared for the President's Commission on Violence, Cleveland police are severely criticized for numerous acts of misbehavior directed not only at black militants but also at black citizens in general during that city's disturbance.[12] In Oakland, California two police officers on duty, in uniform and intoxicated, shot up the headquarters of the Black Panther Party. In Brooklyn, New York, a group of off-duty policemen attacked several Black Panthers with rubber hoses in a Federal Court building.[13] In Chicago, according to another report prepared for the President's Commission on Violence, police activities during convention week

[11] See Louis H. Masotti and Jerome R. Corsi, *Shoot-out in Glenville: The Escalation of Civil Violence: Cleveland, July 23–28, 1968.* A report to the National Commission on the Causes and Prevention of Violence, November 15, 1968.

[12] *Ibid.*

[13] See the Report of the Task Force on Demonstrations, Protests and Group Violence, National Commission on Causes and Prevention of Violence, by Jerome Skolnick, et al., 1969.

constituted a "police riot."[14] And in the fall of the year, the *New York Times* exposed a police practice known as 'cooping,' where policemen find comfortable places to sleep while on duty during the late night-early morning shifts.[15] Given the level of public concern about 'law and order,' reinforced by constantly rising crime statistics, and promoted as an issue in the 1968 presidential campaign by both Richard Nixon and third party candidate George Wallace, none of these practices by urban police departments enhances public confidence in their ability to provide adequate and impartial protection. Many urban residents, both black and white, have begun to fear the cop almost as much as the criminal.

The term "black power" was coined by Stokely Carmichael in 1966, but in its self-help, self-respect and racial pride aspects, the concept can be traced at least as far back as Booker T. Washington and Marcus Garvey. Without doubt there has been a strong movement in the direction of black unity in the interest of black power. In the process, severe conflicts and anxieties both within the black community and between it and its erstwhile allies in the civil rights struggle have developed. In effect, black power is the antithesis of the essential thrust of the integration-oriented civil rights movement until the mid-1960's. But black power and its implied self-segregation, at least as an immediate strategy, seem to have taken hold in black communities throughout the nation. Most whites and many blacks associate the term with anti-white violence, a view reinforced by the virulent and aggressive statements of such black leaders as Stokely Carmichael, H. Rap Brown ("kill whitey"), and some leaders of the Black Panther Party like Bobbie Seale ("We hate you white people!"). To others black power means black capitalism, or more precisely, green power for black people. Perhaps the best example of this is former football star Jimmy Brown's Black Economic Union, which helps to establish black entrepreneurs. More recently black capitalism has gained considerable attention as President Nixon's solution for the racial crisis. Critics, however, point out that black capitalism, like any other capitalism, tends to create a bourgeois elite without helping the masses. For still others, black power means the trappings of blackness—African styled garments and

[14] Daniel Walker, *op cit.*
[15] *New York Times*, December 10, 1968, p. 1.

'natural' hair-dos. Or black power may mean a voluntary physical segregation of blacks from whites, which may take the form of 'community control,' as in the struggle for black autonomy in the New York City public school system, or a religious experience with social and economic overtones of voluntary segregation as with the Black Muslims. For still others it represents a total separation from a dominant white society. Garvey's plan to transplant American Negroes to an African state finds its contemporary analogy in proposals to take over several southern states for black Americans, in Floyd McKissick's proposal to build a "Soul City" in North Carolina, or even in Eric Hoffer's somewhat facetious suggestion that Nevada be given to Negroes for self-improvement and development. But a recent CBS News Survey on white and Negro attitudes toward race-related issues and activities did not find much support for black separatism among either Negroes or whites.[16] Interestingly, whites proved much more supportive of proposals to create a separate nation for Negroes within the United States (twenty-three per cent to three per cent), and a separate country for Negroes outside the United States (thirty-three per cent to five per cent). A survey in New York City among black parents of students attending experimental black controlled school districts found them split fifty-fifty on the plan.

Each of these concepts of black power echoes a central theme of black identity and racial pride. But none appear to have overwhelming, and perhaps not even majority, support among the black population. The stresses and strains of shifting from integration to a voluntary segregation strategy raise questions for both blacks and whites, neither of whom is quite sure of the implications.

The black power movement has had and continues to have a deleterious effect on the black-white coalition which gave direction to the civil rights struggle. As black power replaces racial integration as the dominant strategy in the Negro community, many old-line Negro leaders and almost all the white liberal leaders find themselves struggling for power and relevance in a rapidly changing situation. But probably no single group of the Negroes' erstwhile allies in the civil rights struggle has been hurt as badly as the Jews. Blacks accuse them of economically exploiting the Negro

[16] CBS News, *White and Negro Attitudes towards Race Related Issues and Activities*, Public Opinion Survey, July 9, 1968.

in the ghetto, where Jewish shopkeepers and landlords remained long after their neighbors had moved out, and of thwarting black progress in ghetto schools where Jewish teachers and administrators hinder black assertion and community control. But blatant black anti-Semitic attacks such as the black teacher on a New York City radio station reading a student paper concluding that "the Nazis didn't kill enough of you Jews," do not improve the situation.

Jews could not and have not remained stoical. One leading Jewish leader has stated that "the damage done to Negro-Jewish relations in some of our major urban areas is already beyond early repair." He concluded that the significant deterioration of white-Negro relations since the report of the Kerner Commission "must be laid ... not primarily to white but to black racism. Polarization has escalated in frightening tempo."[17]

The black power movement did not initiate and is not the sole cause of campus violence, but black power and black students have played a significant role in the escalation of violence on the college campus, and even more so in the violence spreading through urban public school systems. Even without large numbers of black students, the college campus shares the crisis of authority with other American institutions. Until relatively recently violence on college and university campuses has tended to be of the 'innocent' type, i.e., students 'letting off steam.' However, the major outbreak at the University of California at Berkeley in 1964 signalled a new development in campus violence which has since grown in scope and intensity. Students have increased their protest against university rules and regulations, against administrators, against university actions and/or inactions in the community, and against the war in Vietnam generally and on specific issues (e.g., ROTC units and recruiting on campus by war-related industries).[18] The most recent wave of campus violence seems to focus on demands for more black studies programs and black faculty for the growing number of black students. In some cases the demands in-

---

[17] Hyman Bookbinder, quoted in the *New York Times*, February 6, 1969.

[18] One study on 19th and 20th century student movements has concluded that all student uprisings are a form of "symbolic parricide" in which a young generation tries to humiliate and overthrow the institutions of its parents regardless of the political issues or consequences. See Lewis Feuer, *The Conflict of Generations* (New York: Basic Books, 1969).

clude the establishment of a black college within the university, degree granting programs in black studies, and power to select faculty and run programs.

At the high school level the problems are similar, with students demanding more relevant curricula and protesting the arbitrary and ambiguous exercise of authority by school officials. In racially-integrated schools sporadic but serious outbreaks of racial violence occur and many now maintain police patrols in the halls. The blackboard jungle has become another piece of the mosaic of civil disorder and disruption in American society.

Thus far the crisis of authority and the questioning of legitimacy has resulted in separate polarizations within organizational and institutional structures. As yet the coalition of the alienated—a coalition which is historically necessary for revolution—does not exist. Black power challenges urban institutions, the peace movement confronts foreign policy makers, advocates of the 'new politics' shake the political parties, clergymen chastise their churches, and students disrupt the campus and create disorder in the classroom. There is conflict and disorder with a common theme of questioned legitimacy all about us, but there is no single issue or cause to unify the dissidents. Whether this series of individual polarizations remains separate depends in large part on the perceptions and reactions of the majority public and its officials. When protesting groups succeed in communicating their grievances, confrontation can be avoided and legitimacy reestablished only if the response is appropriate and creative. All too often, however, the response to protest, even when the grievances are legitimate, is the immediate resort to counterviolence and repression. While it *may* restore order, it will escalate violence and increase polarization. Robert Cipes makes the point well:

> The real danger of the Negro riots is the response they will produce from the forces of "law and order." Repression of riots has already caused more loss of life than the riots themselves. Historically the worst atrocities have been committed not against but in the name of public security.[19]

[19] Robert M. Cipes, *The Crime War* (New York: New American Library, 1968), p. xii.

Order can be maintained either by repressive force or by consensus based on a shared sense of justice and responsible behavior by those in power. Laws apply not only to black citizens but to white citizens and public officials. Whites who practice racism—blatant or subtle—and politicians who promise everything and deliver nothing create the same environment for disorder as those who resort to civil violence. Agents of social control—the police, prosecutors, and even judges—who ignore not only the spirit but often the letter of the law are as lawless and disorderly as the ghetto resident who riots. The rhetoric of justice and equality requires the development of attitudes, behavior and policies to match. Otherwise the frustration of rising expectations, which undermines legitimacy, can only promote the conditions for violence and even revolution.

The dominant white society has thus far been unwilling, although certainly not unable, to do what was necessary to create a nation which practices its eloquent ideology. When blacks were obsequious, whites exploited them; when blacks protested nonviolently, whites cursed and clobbered them; and when blacks resorted to the ultimate resource, violence, whites have repressed them. Because white Americans still refuse to listen, black Americans have begun to look to themselves for answers. But even as the polarization increases, progress toward justice and equality is being made. It may be, however, a case of too little and too late. It becomes increasingly doubtful that the option of effective action to avoid apartheid in America is open. But if this option is closed, a beginning of the end of American racial violence is nowhere in sight and the 'time to burn' has only begun.

INDEX

INDEX

PRINTED IN U.S.A.

DATE DUE